the UNCONVENTIONAL CEO

HOW TO BUILD
WEALTH & **JOY**
IN THE FACE OF ADVERSITY

W0006189

Ruby "SunShine" Taylor

Edited by Ashley Orman

Book cover design by Heather Lawver from Perfectly Pitched

ISBN 978-0-9745122-9-7

www.FinancialJoySchool.com
www.UnConventionalCEO.com

Dedication

This book is lovingly dedicated to my dear parents, Martin and Arline Taylor, and to all those who strive for financial empowerment and a brighter tomorrow.

TABLE OF CONTENTS

Foreword 9

Introduction 11

PART 1: OVERCOMING ADVERSITY AND BUILDING RESILIENCE

Overcoming Financial Trauma...19

Unraveling Financial Trauma and the Impact on Relationships...27

The Racial Wealth Gap and Its Impact on My Family................35

The Resilience Factor: Bouncing Back from Financial

    Trauma & Hardship..42

PART 2: BUILDING GENERATIONAL WEALTH

Directing My Money – The Anti-Budget Revolution 55

Fostering a Wealth Mindset: The Key to Financial

    Empowerment...62

Breaking News … You Don't Have to Be Rich to Build

    Generational Wealth 68

Balancing Financial Styles in a Relationship................................77

The Building Blocks of Investing: The Top 15 Terms You

    Need to Know 81

Investing $100 – A Step-by-Step Guide 86

Crafting Our Legacy: Building Generational Wealth..................92

Protecting Your Legacy: Why You Need a Will and

    Living Trust...98

INTERMISSION

Rising Above Hardship with Faith and Love –
  My Mother's Story 107
Embracing Change and Finding Purpose 114
Charting a New Course: Navigating the Finance Industry 121
"A Journey of Resilience, Leadership, and Success" 129

PART 3: THE UNCONVENTIONAL CEO: LEADING THE WAY

I Am an UnConventional CEO 137
Your Road Map to Resilience, Wealth, and Leadership:
  Practical Steps and Action Plans 143
The Realities and Triumphs of Entrepreneurship and
  Leadership 150
Embracing Joy in Your Life: Understanding the Power of
  Your Inner Light 157
Resources for Financial Education, Mentorship,
  and Entrepreneurial Support 165
My Resilience, Sunshine, and a Personal Mission for Change ...171

About the Author 177
Acknowledgments 181

Foreword

*A*s a retired NFL player, I've had my share of adversities, both on and off the field. And if there's one thing I've learned, it's that success is as much about resilience and mindset as it is about physical strength and skill. That's why I'm excited to introduce you to *The UnConventional CEO: How to Build Wealth and Joy in the Face of Adversity*, a book by my good friend Ruby Taylor.

Ruby's journey is unconventional, to say the least. From overcoming personal obstacles to defying societal norms, Ruby has blazed a unique trail to success. And the best part? She has shared her wisdom, insights, and strategies in this book, creating a blueprint for anyone seeking to redefine their path and find joy amid adversity.

The UnConventional CEO isn't only about building wealth. It's about creating a life of purpose, happiness, and impact. It's about understanding that our actions can help bridge gaps in our society, like the racial wealth gap, and bring about real, meaningful change.

I believe this book will inspire, challenge, and equip you with the tools to become the best version of yourself. Whether you're an aspiring entrepreneur, a seasoned professional, or someone looking for a fresh perspective on success, this book is for you.

So, join me in this transformative journey. Embrace the unconventional. Redefine success on your terms. And let's build wealth and joy together in the face of adversity.

Ryan Broyles, Former NFL and Oklahoma star football player turned real estate developer

Introduction

*H*AVE YOU EVER felt overwhelmed by life's challenges and obstacles? Do you struggle to see a path toward financial stability and wealth building, even with your glasses on? If so, it's time to embrace your inner Unconventional CEO.

It's time to take control of your life, your finances, and your destiny. Welcome to the world of the Unconventional CEO.

My name is Ruby "SunShine" Taylor, and I am an UnConventional CEO here to guide you on this transformative journey. As a survivor of a traumatic brain injury and a passionate advocate for closing the racial wealth gap, I have experienced firsthand the challenges and barriers that stand in the way of financial freedom. But I refuse to let adversity define me. Instead, I have embraced an UnConventional path that defies expectations and blazes a trail toward joy, financial stability, and generational wealth.

Like most Americans, I thought I had it all figured out. I would work hard, retire early, and travel the world. It was a simple plan, but one I believed in wholeheartedly. However, life has a funny way of throwing us curveballs when we least expect them. In 2012, my life took a sharp turn, and the future I had envisioned for myself began to unravel.

It started with a seemingly ordinary day. I had enjoyed a trip to Walmart and indulged in a meal from Boston Market (nothing but the best for me, I joked). But on my way home, I was involved in a devastating car accident that changed my life forever. The crash left me with a traumatic brain injury, forcing me to stop working as a school social worker.

As someone with no income and from a family not privy to generational wealth, I was in a health and financial crisis. The threat of homelessness loomed over me as my life and finances spiraled out of control. As a tenured educator with union support, I assumed I would be provided everything in my contract. However, as many African Americans know, rules and contracts sometimes fail to protect us. This left me without insurance or income for months. My parents unable to pay my mortgage and condo fees without putting themselves in financial jeopardy, and I felt like a lone wolf with no savings, investments, or financial support to turn to.

I felt overwhelmed, scared, and unsure of how to move forward. Everything I had worked so hard for seemed to slip through my fingers. Yet, as I struggled to make sense of my new reality, I discovered a resilience I didn't know I possessed inside me. This resilience would ultimately become the driving force that propelled me forward, helping me to find new ways to overcome adversity and rebuild my life.

During this challenging time, I took a deep dive into my finances and searched for answers and solutions. I realized that to bounce back, I needed to learn how to grow my money, invest wisely, and create a financial safety net for myself. As I began educating myself about financial education and wealth building, I discovered I wasn't alone. In my experience, many people, particularly those from Black and Brown communities, face similar challenges. We often lack the essential knowledge and resources to break through financial barriers and attain financial freedom.

This realization ignited a fire within me. I was determined to regain control of my financial future and help others do the same. And so, with unwavering determination and a newfound sense of purpose, I embarked on a journey to create a platform that would empower Black and Brown youth and families with the knowledge and tools we need to build wealth and find joy in the face of adversity.

The UnConventional CEO: How to Build Wealth and Joy in the Face of Adversity is the story of my journey—a journey filled with obstacles, setbacks, and triumphs. It is a testament to the power of resilience, the importance of financial education, and the unwavering belief that even in our darkest moments, a ray of sunshine awaits you.

In these pages, you will join me as I navigate the challenges of rebuilding my life and discover the unconventional strategies that have helped me survive and thrive. I will share practical insights, personal anecdotes, and valuable lessons learned. Together, we will explore the intersection of resilience, financial empowerment, and personal fulfillment, unlocking the secrets to building wealth and finding joy in adversity.

I invite you to embark on this transformative journey with me. Challenge the status quo, rewrite the rules, and embrace your role as UnConventional CEO. Together, we will uncover the untapped potential within ourselves and our communities. We will shatter the limitations imposed by systemic oppression and rewrite our narratives of success and abundance.

As you read this book, I want you to remember that you shape your destiny. You are the CEO of your life, your family, your community, and our global world. Embrace your resilience. Harness the knowledge you've gained, and take bold action toward your financial goals and leadership abilities. Believe in your ability to overcome obstacles. You can create a life of abundance and joy.

Your journey doesn't end here. It's just the beginning. I encourage you to share your newfound knowledge and empower others on their path to financial freedom and leadership. Let's uplift marginalized communities, dismantle the barriers to wealth creation, and create a future where everyone has equal opportunities to thrive.

Thank you for joining me on this transformative journey. I am filled with hope and excitement for the future we are building together. Remember, the UnConventional CEO within you is ready to make a lasting impact. Now go forth and unleash your financial potential, create generational wealth, and spread joy throughout your life and beyond.

With love, resilience, and unwavering determination, never give up on your dreams …

Ruby "SunShine" Taylor, MSW

"The content provided by Ruby 'SunShine' Taylor is intended for educational purposes only and should not be considered as personalized financial advice."

Overcoming
Adversity and
Building Resilience

Overcoming Financial Trauma

*F*INANCIAL TRAUMA CAN pose a formidable challenge in pursuing financial stability, contentment, and success. Navigating through the turbulent waters of financial trauma can be as uncomfortable as stepping on a Lego barefoot— far from the American dream. In my experience, the racial wealth gap has been a consistent source of financial trauma, and to be frank, it continues to be. The racial wealth gap looms like an unwelcome guest who lingers for too long, more persistent than a politician wanting reelection. One of the most challenging financial traumas I've encountered was after a car accident in 2012 that left me with a traumatic brain injury. You're probably now scratching your head, questioning, "What does a car accident have to do with a racial wealth gap?" I completely get it. Keep reading.

The traumatic brain injury left me unable to work, plunging me into an uncertain financial situation. The aftermath temporarily stole my ability to work, pitching me into financial unpredictability. Yet, the relentless support of my family, community, and medical team, and the invaluable wisdom shared by friends like Renee and her husband, Dan, paved the path to my financial recovery, and more importantly, to emotional and mental stability. How did I land in such a financial crisis? Let's rewind a bit. Immersed in my role as a school social worker, I cherished every moment with my students and their families. If you're imagining a plush salary, think again. My salary was in the high millions—of smiles, not dollars! Every day, I was knee-deep in the dazzling world of students and their families. Stationed in Lancaster, Pennsylvania, I was blessed to be part of a community so loving, they'd give your favorite aunt a run for her money. And religious? We had more faith than Noah building his ark!

In my role, I had the privilege of supporting these mini movers and shakers in their educational journey and personal growth, a task that filled my cup to the brim with fulfillment. The best part of waking up is having purpose in your cup— OK, I apologize for the unexpected commercial break, but I couldn't resist!

Throughout my career, which spanned over a decade, my belief was simple: You can't fully uplift a young person without also lending a hand to their families. This mantra had me clocking more hours in living rooms and dining rooms, providing guidance and support to families in their hour of need. And you know what? I wouldn't trade a single minute of it, no matter what my bank account whispered, **"Limited funds, caution, use wisely."**

The truth is: My generosity didn't stop at giving my time. Nope, I also dipped into my own resources to support my students and their families when they found themselves in a financial crisis. But why stop there? My family also benefited from my giving nature. It's the Southern way, after all—at least, that's what I believed then.

Although, I've since realized some "Southern ways" are better left in the past. We're talking about the likes of slavery, rocking plaid in the blistering summer, and poorly lit highways. There are many more, but our time is limited.

Now, let's get back to the Lancaster community. It was a melting pot of diverse cultures, beliefs, and backgrounds, providing a rich environment for learning and personal growth.

Despite many of these families' challenges, there was a strong sense of unity. This support system was essential in helping each family navigate their unique circumstances and become more resilient in the face of adversity.

The love and care I poured into my work would eventually come back to me in ways I could never have anticipated. When I could no longer work due to my traumatic brain injury, two parents of my former students, Jeremiah and Kenyon, stepped in to provide unwavering support. They drove me to doctor appointments, took me out to lunch, helped with grocery shopping, made me dinner, and even assisted me in going to purchase my new car. The love, support, and guidance I had given to so many families over the years were now being returned to me when I needed it most.

During this period of vulnerability, I began to understand the power of community. The kindness and generosity of the people around me helped me through my recovery and provided valuable lessons that would shape the rest of my life.

One day, a parent named Renee Gallagher took me out to lunch. As we talked, I opened up about my fears of losing my condo and becoming homeless. She asked me where my savings and investments were, knowing that as a school social worker, I had earned a decent salary. I sheepishly admitted that I had none. Renee's response was simple but powerful: "You're never supposed to spend your last dime." These words would become a guiding principle in my life.

Renee and her husband were long-term investors, and they graciously offered to teach me how to invest so I would never find myself in such an uncertain position again. They invited me to their beautiful, well-manicured mansion, where they shared their financial wisdom with me. I was wondering if I became homeless would they let me stay here? Just a quick thought and back to reality I went.

Over several weeks, they taught me a new language and opened my eyes to how money works. Just like any new language, foreign concepts can be uncomfortable and hard to learn but once you get it, a new perspective begins. The beauty of discovery blossoms like a tiger lily. I know very poetic; that is the money side coming out of me, sounding like a French poet. I learned about compound interest, investing, the differences between long- and short-term investments (and the perils of short-term thinking), brokerage accounts, brokerage firms, and much more. Their education and support set me on a new financial trajectory.

While learning about personal finance and investing, I discovered that many families, including mine, faced similar challenges. A lack of investing education and awareness about growing money beyond traditional employment left us susceptible to financial hardships. Inspired by the help I received, I became determined to use my newfound knowledge to help others in my community become more financially resilient and secure.

This experience taught me several valuable lessons: I should never spend my last dime; instead, I should invest and save my money for the long term. Life does get better, and the tragedies we face can lead to valuable lessons that help us grow and empower others. The power of community is an incredible force that can help individuals overcome adversity and develop the resilience needed to thrive.

But let's be clear: overcoming financial trauma is not a quick fix or an overnight process. It requires a commitment to change, a willingness to learn, and the support of those around you. It's about reevaluating your relationship with money, challenging long-held beliefs, and adopting new strategies that set you on a path toward financial well-being.

In the following chapters, I will share the insights and strategies I learned from Renee and her husband, as well as my own journey toward financial resilience and success. When you complete this book, you'll have gained insight into financial investing and why being an UnConventional CEO empowers communities.

However, it's crucial to understand that financial trauma extends beyond personal experiences. It is deeply rooted in systemic inequalities and historic injustices. The racial wealth gap, for example, has perpetuated financial trauma among marginalized communities, particularly African American families. The legacy of slavery, segregation, discriminatory practices, and limited access to opportunities has created significant barriers to wealth accumulation and financial stability. I can't say this enough.

To truly overcome financial trauma, we must address these systemic issues and advocate for economic justice and equality. This involves fighting for fair wages, affordable housing, equitable education, access to capital and resources, and dismantling the structures that perpetuate the racial wealth gap.

Alongside policy changes, it's about empowering individuals with the knowledge and tools to navigate the financial landscape and build generational wealth. Investing in financial education and financial programs can provide individuals with the skills and confidence to make informed financial decisions, break the cycle of economic trauma, and create a brighter future for themselves and their families.

As we embark on this journey together, I encourage you to reflect on your own financial experiences and the impact they have had on your life. Consider the systemic factors that may have contributed to your financial trauma, or financial privilege. Let's work together to promote healing, challenge these barriers, and create a more inclusive and equitable financial system.

Overcoming financial trauma is not an easy task, but it is indeed possible to triumph over it. It takes reflection, prayer, wisdom, resilience, education, and a supportive community. By coming together, we can rewrite the narrative, shatter the chains of financial trauma, and lay the foundation for a future where everyone can thrive.

Unraveling Financial Trauma and the Impact on Relationships

GROWING UP, I witnessed the tremendous financial stress endured by my hardworking parents. While they were able to navigate the challenges of living within their means, many other family members faced the constant struggle of living paycheck to paycheck. However, despite their financial constraints, my parents' unwavering generosity and sense of responsibility toward family and community only added to their financial burdens.

I observed firsthand their selfless support and provision of resources to loved ones facing financial challenges. These experiences opened my eyes to the profound impact of financial trauma on marginalized communities. In some communities, where generational wealth is absent and resources are limited, breaking free from the cycle of poverty becomes more arduous. It is a constant struggle to find stability and create opportunities for a better future because the need to assist our loved ones takes precedence over growing wealth.

Unfortunately, the communal nature of resource sharing often leads to a paradoxical outcome. When one person within the community manages to get ahead financially, their success is short-lived as their resources become communal property. This dynamic creates a complex web in which progress is difficult to sustain, and individuals find themselves constantly caught in a cycle of giving and rarely receiving.

Within my family, the collective well-being has always been prioritized over individual wealth. This often resulted in the allocation of extra resources to family or community members in need, even when our own financial stability was at risk. The belief that money holds more value when used to assist others rather than when it is allowed to accumulate became deeply ingrained in me and instantly connected to my sense of self-worth or lack thereof.

My parents taught me the importance of prioritizing family and community over personal financial and emotional well-being. While community economics can be a blessing when everyone contributes to the pot, it becomes burdensome and perpetuates further financial trauma when only one family or person carries the weight of the entire family. This dynamic creates a limited understanding of self-worth and reinforces the transactional nature of relationships, where the feel-good aspect of money exchange overshadows the importance of genuine connections.

The far-reaching impact of financial trauma on my family and countless others underscores the urgent need to address the racial wealth gap and create equitable opportunities. It is crucial to confront systemic barriers, advocate for policies that promote economic equality, and provide resources and support to marginalized communities. By addressing these issues, we can break the financial trauma cycle and empower individuals and families to build a brighter future.

It is essential to explore the concept of financial trauma and its effects on oppressed communities, particularly for African Americans like me. Our relationship with money, as well as the trauma associated with it, is deeply rooted in our shared history of slavery and oppression. For centuries, our ancestors were denied the right to possess money and were treated as property, valuable enough to be assets to others but not valuable enough to possess wealth themselves. This perspective laid the groundwork for the financial trauma experienced by my family, which continues to impact us today.

Through reflecting on my past, it becomes evident how the financial trauma experienced by my family has profoundly influenced our relationships. We have fallen into the trap of transactional relationships, where money and resources serve as the primary basis for connection. This pattern has become deeply ingrained in our lives, reinforcing the narrative that our worth is defined solely by external measures. Unfortunately, this emphasis on transactional connections undermines the significance of genuine relationships built on unconditional love, support, and shared experiences.

One aspect that stands out is the realization that certain individuals would only reach out to us when they were in need. We rarely saw them unless they required something from us. This experience became ingrained in me and shaped my perception of relationships. It created a belief that in order for people to be present in my life, I must provide them with something they need, whether it's free labor, money, or other forms of assistance. This dynamic further fueled my financial trauma, as it reinforced the notion that my value as a person was contingent on what I could offer materialistically.

This understanding highlights the damaging effects of transactional relationships and the way it perpetuates the cycle of financial trauma. It becomes a constant struggle to differentiate between genuine connections and those driven by personal gain. It also makes saving money difficult to impossible because every extra dime goes toward a loved one in need. As I continue my journey of healing and growth, I am committed to breaking free from this pattern and redefining my relationships based on authentic connections rather than the exchange of material resources.

It was not until my college years, when my friend Lori staged a one-woman intervention, that I even began to question the nature of my actions. One day walking around campus on our way back to our dorm, I said, "Lori, I will give you ten dollars if you walk with me to 7-Eleven." She gave me a puzzled look, her brow furrowing in confusion. "Why do you always feel the need to shell out money just for someone to hang out with you?" she asked. Her question struck me like a bolt out of the blue. It's not like I transformed overnight—after all, the Pyramids weren't built in a day. Still, her words sowed a seed deep within me, one that would need time, trials, and tribulations to fully blossom.

Fast forward a few decades, and the proverbial light bulb clicked, illuminating a truth I had long been blind to—my worth as a person isn't tied to my financial status. It's not measured in dollar signs or the balance in my bank account. I have come to a profound realization that my worth extends far beyond monetary contributions. It encompasses my presence, experiences, wisdom, love, and capacity for healing. And boy, did that realization hit harder than a Pepsi on ice!

Financial trauma is a potent brew, spiced with a long-standing legacy of systemic racism and discriminatory practices. It's a cocktail that my family and countless others have been forced to swallow. This unfortunate concoction has done more than drain bank accounts—it's sown a seed of unworthiness and fostered a scarcity mindset within many African American families, including my own.

The financial trauma caused by the racial wealth gap extends beyond immediate economic struggles and seeps into mental health, relationships, and overall well-being. Those who have experienced financial trauma often develop a sense of self-worth based on external measures such as degrees, possessions, and access, constantly worrying about money and finding it difficult to trust others or plan for the future. The intergenerational nature of this trauma further compounds its effects, as emotional and psychological burdens are passed down through the generations.

In my family's history, the gnarled roots of financial trauma run as deep as an ancient oak. The historical and systemic roadblocks that obstructed our pathway to wealth accumulation have left us, like a ship without a compass, exposed, without a safety net or fertile ground for growth. It's a burdensome yoke my siblings frequently bear, feeling ensnared in a relentless cycle of financial adversity. Some have even internalized a profound sense of unworthiness, viewing themselves not as potential providers but as burdens on our family's financial landscape.

When my father battles to keep up with the bills, at eighty-six-years-old (don't worry about my age, stay focused on the story), his eyes transform into two glowing rubies—a stark indication of blood pressure surging like mercury in a thermometer. The squeeze of scarcity catapults our family back into an era when merely setting foot in certain areas could lead to physical assault or even worse, solely due to the hue of our skin.

Heartbreakingly, it seems those times have never really left us. Our financial trauma is a legacy, stemming from those historical obstacles that have thwarted wealth accumulation and resource transfer among some African American families. Yet, amid this turbulent sea, I've stumbled on a profound epiphany: My worth expands way beyond the confines of my financial contributions. It spans across my presence, my experiences, the wisdom I've gleaned, the love I've shared, and my capacity for healing. The road to financial resilience and healing is akin to climbing a mountain—not without its trials and tribulations. Still, armed with awareness, compassion, and collective action, we have the power to mold a society that is genuinely just, inclusive, and economically empowering for all.

This journey calls on us to confront our past, scrutinize the present, and conjure a future where economic opportunities aren't shackled by race or systemic disadvantages. So, let's embark on this transformative odyssey toward financial liberation, where our worth isn't gauged by the figures in our bank accounts but by the love, wisdom, and resilience we sprinkle in our world.

And with that, dear reader, we close this chapter, but the narrative is far from over. There are still stories to unravel, lessons to learn, and battles to conquer. Keep those pages turning, our journey is just beginning.

The Racial Wealth Gap and Its Impact on My Family

*T*HE IMPACT OF the racial wealth gap on my family and millions of other African American and marginalized families is profound and far-reaching. It is a result of a long history of systemic racism, which includes the legacies of slavery, Jim Crow laws, redlining, and the ongoing effects of discrimination. These historical injustices have created a deeply entrenched disparity in wealth and resources between White families and families of color, perpetuating a cycle of financial struggle and limited opportunities.

For my family, the consequences of the racial wealth gap have been devastating and deeply personal. One of the most tragic events that underscored the far-reaching impact of systemic racism and the racial wealth gap was the murder of my sixteen-year-old brother on the streets of the Bronx, our community. His life was cut short by violence that was, in part, a consequence of the limited opportunities and resources available to us as a result of systemic oppression. How so?

I couldn't help but wonder: If our community had been given equal access to opportunities, resources, and generational wealth like other communities, would my brother's murderer and his friend have felt the need to turn to violence? What if we had grown up in a non-racist and just world, free from the burdens of discriminatory practices such as redlining and the detrimental effects of strategically introduced drugs and guns in our communities? What if we had access to great schools and lived in safe neighborhoods? These questions are painful to contemplate as they bring to light the deep impact of the racial wealth gap and systemic oppression on our lives.

The racial wealth gap is not merely an abstract concept; it has tangible and lasting effects on families like mine. The historical context of slavery, in which African Americans were treated as property and denied access to economic opportunity, has left a deep imprint on our collective psyche. The trauma of our ancestors' enslavement and subsequent systemic oppression continues to reverberate across generations, shaping our experiences with money, success, and self-worth.

The legacy of slavery was followed by the era of Jim Crow laws, which further reinforced racial segregation and economic disparities. African Americans were systematically denied access to quality education, fair employment, and the ability to accumulate wealth. These discriminatory practices laid the foundation for the racial wealth gap, setting the stage for my family's challenges.

Redlining, another egregious practice, further exacerbated the racial wealth gap by denying African American families access to housing loans and investment opportunities in certain neighborhoods. This discriminatory practice deprived families of the chance to build wealth through homeownership and perpetuated segregation and limited access to resources, including quality education and health care.

These historical injustices have profoundly impacted my family's financial journey. The lack of generational wealth, compounded by limited access to good education, fair wages, and investment opportunities, left us vulnerable and without a safety net. Despite my parents' relentless hard work and determination to provide for us, the uphill battle to build generational wealth sometimes felt insurmountable.

I vividly recall my parents' stories of growing up as the children of sharecroppers in the backwoods of North Carolina, where my roots come from. They worked tirelessly on the farm, endured long hours, all while being cheated out of fair payment. Their parents, my grandparents, struggled to make ends meet and provide for their families under the weight of systemic discrimination. The cycle of poverty and limited opportunities seemed unbreakable. So, my parents changed their location separately and moved to New York City for better opportunities, where they encountered similar mistreatment and systemic barriers. They were consistently undervalued and underpaid, despite their hard work and dedication. However, they made much more in NYC than North Carolina, which afforded them more financial opportunities. Their extra resources forced them to extend themselves financially to help family and friends.

It became evident that the racial wealth gap, which has its roots in historical and systemic oppression, profoundly impacted my family's journey. The barriers to wealth accumulation that my ancestors faced continued to shape our experiences, constraining our access to resources, homes, and perpetuating financial instability.

These systemic barriers and the weight of the racial wealth gap have also had a profound impact on my own financial journey. As a school social worker, I dedicated myself to supporting my family, students, and their families. However, when a life-altering car accident left me unable to work, I found myself without savings, investments, or the safety net of family financial support. The absence of generational wealth, directly linked to the historical and ongoing effects of the racial wealth gap, left me vulnerable and on the brink of homelessness.

But how did I land myself in this predicament? It was a vicious circle of aiding others without possessing the right resources and knowledge to safeguard myself. Lacking the cushion of generational wealth, I was all too familiar with the gnawing pit of financial struggle. It was this bitter experience, coupled with my upbringing, that fueled my desire to give to my family and my students' families in times of need.

As a Black woman, I know firsthand what it's like when bills start to resemble a pack of hungry wolves eyeing your paycheck like it's the last piece of meat. You're left feeling as hopeless as a fish on a bicycle, with nobody to turn to for help. Your own family can't lend a hand because they're battling their own financial monsters, and the government deems you too "well-off" to qualify for assistance.

This, my friends, is a front-row seat view of how the racial wealth gap took a chunk out of my financial stability. It's like having your cake and watching someone else eat it. Not a pretty sight, huh?

The consequences of the racial wealth gap extend beyond financial struggles. The psychological burden of financial insecurity, coupled with the awareness that our struggles are a result of systemic discrimination, can lead to feelings of frustration, despair, and hopelessness. These emotions became woven into the fabric of my relationships, as I often felt the need to use money to validate my worth and secure connections with others, mirroring the transactional nature of survival in a racially unequal society.

So, there you have it, folks. The racial wealth gap isn't just some abstract idea debated in ivory towers or the fodder for prime-time news; it's as real as the ground we stand on. This harsh reality has been the unseen hand shaping the lives and fortunes of African American families for generations. It's like an unwanted inheritance, passed down through the years, silently and persistently.

This wealth gap didn't just magically appear out of nowhere. It's the offspring of historical and current practices that have systematically denied Black families the golden ticket to wealth accumulation, a ticket their White counterparts often take for granted—like a devious game of musical chairs, where the music never stops, and the chairs are always just out of reach.

This systemic injustice has spun a web of limited resources, turning access to quality education and health care into a high-stakes lottery. Economic mobility? That's become as elusive as a unicorn sighting, all thanks to this persistent wealth gap.

So, as we close this chapter, remember: The racial wealth gap is more than just numbers and statistics. It's about real people with real dreams, aspirations, and potential. It's about families that work hard and play by the rules yet find the goalposts constantly moving.

But this isn't where our story ends. Oh no, we're just getting started. Keep turning those pages, because the next chapter promises more twists, turns, and maybe even a few surprises. Buckle up, because this ride is far from over!

The Resilience Factor: Bouncing Back from Financial Trauma & Hardship

*D*URING MY JOURNEY of healing, I composed a poem titled "Brain Injury." Would you like to hear it? Here it goes:

No matter how hard I pressed the brakes and tried to turn, Life would not stop or give me a break.

As my car was forced to hit another car, which turned in front of me,

Life would not stop.

No matter how much I thought I don't have enough sick days to take leave,

Life would not stop.

A few days is all you need, that's what my doctors said to me,

Life would not stop.

A few days turned into a few weeks, a few weeks turned into a few months, and a few months turned into two years, and the words I knew were coming, I still did not want to hear,

Life would not stop.

"You won't be returning to your career as a school social worker," my doctor said to me.

Life would not stop.

No money in the bank, bills coming every day, and my disability retirement; child, please, that is barely making ends meet,

Life would not stop.

As I try to force this new journey to end, it continues like an overextended commercial forcing me to watch to the very end,

Life would not stop.

Threats of potentially losing my home, unsure what to do or where to turn,

Life would not stop.

As I looked in the mirror and saw a reflection of an enemy I never knew, she was no friend of mine. How can I be friends with a perfect stranger who came into my house and would not leave?

Life would not stop.

The job I gave so much of myself to discriminated against me and prohibited me from returning to school, just to visit my students,

Life would not stop.

Trying to find reasons to smile but unable to feel happiness, just felt down, down, down,

Life would not stop.

Attempting to adjust to the new me, unable to sleep, and every little noise bothering me,

Life would not stop.

But as I continued to breathe, inhaling a mountain-high worth of oxygen, feeling the power of God holding me,

I finally realized, as I exhaled, that I DID NOT STOP, no matter how difficult life was for me.

Life would not stop, and neither will I!

In the words of Langston Hughes, life has not been a crystal stair. For me, life has been like twelve rounds of boxing with Muhammad Ali, followed by another twelve rounds with Floyd Mayweather, and to top it off, three rounds with Mike Tyson.

At the end of those beatdowns, we end with a twenty-one-day cruise around Hawaii, a thirty-day vacation through Africa, and eight days in Disney (after DeSantis leave), all expenses paid. Plus, millions added to my investment accounts, and the world's best hug from the person I love the most, along with affirmations of love and admiration from the person I respect the most. This is how I feel about life—we will get tossed, beat down, and hurt in many rounds, and when we survive it, our dreams we never dreamed become reality, and life begins to feel better for us all. To me, that is resilience—getting beaten up, anticipating great wins, and embracing good times.

According to Ruby's Dictionary (yes, that's me), resilience is the ability to rebound and adapt in the face of adversity. It is crucial when navigating various challenges, including financial trauma. Such difficulties can be particularly daunting, significantly impacting our daily lives, as they often evoke feelings of shame and vulnerability. Overcoming these obstacles can be a formidable task, but with time and effort, resilience can be cultivated and fortified (yep another SAT word, *fortified*).

Let's be real, folks: I can't twiddle my thumbs waiting for the government to swoop in and heroically close the racial wealth gap, creating a fairytale world of financial equity. Sure, that's the expectation. But, as the saying goes, "Hope in one hand, and spit in the other, see which fills up first." Instead of waiting for politicians to miraculously do the right thing (like a scene straight out of a Spike Lee movie), we must step up and shape the world we wish to see. And it all begins within us.

Financial setbacks often create more than just a hole in your pocket—they leave lasting impressions in the form of financial trauma. The kind that messes up our sense of stability and throws roadblocks on our path to opportunity and a prosperous future. These setbacks can generate overwhelming stress and anxiety, making it harder to see the light at the end of the tunnel. However, resilience isn't just about surviving these hardships. It's about tapping into the power within us to overcome them. It's bouncing back from setbacks and finding innovative ways to survive and thrive.

In my personal odyssey, I discovered the strength of resilience in the aftermath of a life-changing car accident. With zero income, empty savings, and no family financial support, I found myself staring down the gaping maw of personal circumstances and the racial wealth gap that had silently shaped my family's financial history. I harnessed the kindness of others and my determination to learn and grow, which fueled my journey back from the brink and pushed me to start rebuilding my best life.

I went through a gut-wrenching period of over two years, grappling with severe financial struggles. My job abruptly stopped paying me, as though they'd hit the pause button without even a heads-up. To add insult to injury, they yanked away my medical benefits, throwing a monkey wrench in my ability to manage my health and well-being. As if things weren't topsy-turvy enough, my water heater staged a rebellion.

It malfunctioned and flooded into my hallway, deepening my financial woes.

I found myself struggling to make ends meet throughout this chaotic roller coaster. I was constantly faced between choosing the worst of two situations: buying necessary medication or securing basic needs such as food. Despite careful juggling, I was slipping and sliding on a financial tightrope.

The financial storm that battered my life whipped up a sea of stress and uncertainty. However, I remained buoyant. I had a relentless determination to navigate my way through. I sought support, dug into available resources, and stood tall through each setback, fueled by a flickering flame of hope for stability and a brighter future.

Resilience isn't just about bouncing back; it's about evolving, becoming stronger, wiser, and more compassionate through the tumult. It's about embracing the storm and emerging on the other side with an increased zest for life and a deeper understanding of our inner fortitude.

Here are some key factors that contributed to my resilience in the face of financial crisis:

Changing Mindsets: Shifting my perspective and recognizing that my financial resources do not define my worth was a transformative moment in my journey. I realized that my relationships shouldn't be solely transactional but instead rooted in genuine connection and mutual support. This shift in mindset allowed me to foster healthier and more meaningful relationships with others. It freed me from the pressure of equating my self-worth with my financial standing and opened up opportunities for personal growth and financial recovery.

Embracing this new mindset was instrumental in my ability to rebuild and thrive, proving that true wealth extends far beyond monetary measures. By adopting a mindset focused on connection, growth, and authenticity, we can cultivate a fulfilling and resilient life that goes beyond financial constraints. As you embark on your own journey, I encourage you to reflect on the nature of your relationships and the underlying beliefs that shape your perspective. Embrace the transformative power of changing mindsets and discovering the joy and abundance of fostering genuine connections, personal growth, and financial recovery.

Fighting for MY Rights: When treated unfairly by my former employer, I needed to stand up for myself and fight for what I have worked for and deserve. By taking legal action and asserting my rights, I was able to secure compensation and send a message that such mistreatment would not be tolerated.

Support Network: The unwavering support of my God, my parents, Renee and Dan, and friends and former students' parents, Melissa and Tony Coleman, played a crucial role in my recovery. They provided the emotional, practical, and financial assistance I needed to overcome challenges and move forward. It's important to remember that it's OK to ask for help and seek support during times of crisis. However, it's equally important to be discerning about the help you receive. As my former student wisely told me, not all help is good help. So, while leaning on your support network, be cautious and selective in accepting assistance. Together, we can navigate the hardships and triumph over adversity with the right people in our corner.

Financial Education: Discovering the principles of long-term investing, compound interest, and other financial concepts transformed my understanding of money and empowered me to make informed financial decisions. It became clear that managing money and growing money are two distinct approaches. Financial education became my compass and guided me toward building wealth and resilience amid economic challenges. It taught me not only how to grow my money but also how to elevate my money management skills and maximize my resources. By embracing financial education, we can pave the way for a brighter financial future and unlock our full potential for financial stability and prosperity.

Advocacy and Community Involvement: Becoming more engaged in advocating for policies and initiatives that promote economic equality and support communities of color has been empowering and helped me connect with others who share similar experiences and goals. This sense of community and purpose can bolster resilience and put your life on a new trajectory.

Adaptability and Resourcefulness: Adapting to new circumstances and finding creative solutions to problems is a cornerstone of resilience. By embracing change and being resourceful, I developed new skills and strategies that have helped me navigate financial challenges and build a more secure future.

Resilience is not a fixed trait; it is a muscle that can be developed and strengthened over time. By cultivating resilience, you can overcome financial hardships and chart a new path toward financial stability and success. Through mindset shifts, support networks, financial education, advocacy, and adaptability, we can bounce back from adversity and create a brighter future for ourselves and our communities yes, YOU.

BUILDING
GENERATIONAL
WEALTH

Directing My Money – The Anti-Budget Revolution

*E*VER SINCE I was knee-high to a grasshopper, the concept of budgeting has been drilled into my head. You know the drill: Pay your bills, cut down on your wants, stash your pennies away for that apocalyptic rainy day. These principles are undeniably important, but they never quite struck a chord with me. And why would they? The entire idea seemed about as appealing as a root canal!

Here I was, trying to make a bid for wealth, and all I was doing was watching my money fly out of the window faster than a kid chasing an ice cream truck. It felt like I was constantly swimming upstream, fighting the current, while also juggling chainsaws. Metaphorically, of course.

So, I decided that enough was enough. There I was, standing at the crossroads, realizing that I needed to dump my old fling with traditional budgeting and look for something … sexier. Something that prioritized growth and wealth building, rather than plugging the drain of outgoing expenses. I wanted my money to work for me, not wave at me as it left my bank account!

And that, dear readers, is when I stumbled on a breakthrough. Call it an epiphany or just too many cups of Pepsi at 2 a.m., but the concept of "directing my money" was born. It was like budgeting but with a dash of fairy dust and a whole lot of joy. Stay tuned, folks.

Things are about to get exciting!

Imagine a leaf caught in the wind, being blown around aimlessly. That was how I felt about my finances before discovering the power of directing my money. I realized that if I don't actively guide my money toward growth and value, it will create chaos instead of stability. I wanted to break free from the constraints of traditional budgeting and focus on building a strong foundation for generational wealth.

In this journey of directing my money, I've realized that the traditional budgeting system doesn't work for everyone. It's time to think differently about our finances and embrace a new approach that prioritizes growth and wealth building. I'm excited to share my experiences with you and, hopefully, inspire you to take control of your finances and direct your money toward a brighter future.

Directing my money is all about taking control of my financial destiny. Instead of just paying off debts and bills, I focus on investing in opportunities that will help my money grow. This shift in mindset has allowed me to approach my finances with a renewed sense of purpose and excitement.

Understanding the difference between secured and unsecured debt is an important aspect of directing my money. While it's crucial to pay off debts, such as a mortgage or car loan, it's equally important to prioritize growing your money. By thinking strategically about debt and evaluating the potential for growth, I can make informed decisions about where to invest my money.

Commitment is key in directing my money. Regardless of the amount, I am dedicated to making my money grow. Whether I can invest a small sum, or a significant amount, consistency and dedication are essential. Investing my money to make more money becomes a priority.

When directing my money, I have a clear order of priorities. First, I direct my money toward necessities like housing, food, medical expenses, and transportation. These are the foundational elements of my financial well-being. I ensure that my basic needs are met and that I have a solid foundation to build on.

Once the essentials are covered, I allocate a portion of my money for enjoyment. I believe life is meant to be enjoyed, and directing my money allows me to do just that. Whether it's treating myself to a vacation, dining out at my favorite restaurant, indulging in a spa day, or attending concerts and events, I make room in my budget for the things that bring me joy. It's about balancing responsible financial management and enjoying the fruits of my labor.

I've also learned the importance of communication in directing my money. If I face financial tightness or unforeseen circumstances, I don't hesitate to contact my credit card companies, lenders, or service providers. I explain my situation and explore potential solutions. They are often willing to work with me, offering flexible payment options or temporary relief. Open and honest communication is key to navigating financial challenges and finding sustainable solutions.

Directing my money is always focused on growth and sustainability. It's about building a strong financial foundation to support me and my loved ones for years. I continuously seek opportunities to invest and grow my wealth. This may involve exploring different investment vehicles, such as stocks, real estate, or starting my own business. I educate myself on financial and investing education, stay updated on market trends, and seek guidance from financial advisors who align with my goals and values.

But directing my money isn't just about accumulating wealth for myself. It's about creating a legacy and generational impact. I believe that wealth should be a tool for positive change and empowerment. As I direct my money, I also prioritize giving back to my community and supporting causes that align with my values. Whether it's donating to charitable organizations, volunteering my time and skills, or mentoring aspiring entrepreneurs, I understand the power of using my financial resources to make a difference.

In the anti-budget revolution, I've discovered the freedom to design my financial path based on my values and aspirations. It's not about strict restrictions or feeling deprived of what I enjoy. Instead, it's about being intentional, purposeful, and mindful about directing my money to create the life I desire. It's a shift in mindset and a commitment to living a life of abundance, both financially and personally.

I invite you to join me on this journey of directing your money. It's time to break free from the limitations of traditional budgeting and embrace a new approach that empowers you to build wealth, pursue your dreams, and make a positive impact in the world. Together, let's rewrite financial management rules and create a future where financial freedom is within reach for everyone. The power to direct your money and shape your financial destiny is in your hands because you are the CEO of your EMPIRE. Are you ready to embark on this revolutionary path to financial abundance and resilience?

FINANCIAL JOY SCHOOL

https://FinancialJoySchool.com

DIRECT YOUR MONEY

Money Coming In

Income	
Business	
Extra	
Total	

Money Grows

Investing	
Bonds	
Saving	
Emergency Fund	
Life Insurance	
Extra	
Total:	

Money Going Out

Housing
(Rent or Mortgage)
Electricity
Gas
Food
Health
Internet
Car Note
Car Insurance
Car Gas
Clothing
Cell Phone
Hair
Traveling
Entertainment
Credit Cards
Loans
Extra's
Total

Money Coming In. [   ] - [   ] **Money Grows =** [   ] - [   ] **Money Going Out. =** [   ] **Total**

Fostering a Wealth Mindset: The Key to Financial Empowerment

MY PERSONAL VOYAGE from a place of "just enough" to a world of "plenty" has revealed to me the extraordinary potential of mindset. An unforeseen brain injury, a life-altering roadblock, not only tested my abilities but forced me to reassess my life. During this life-altering pause, I began reflecting on my mother's awe-inspiring journey from simple beginnings to becoming a triumphant homeowner of three houses. She never doubted her capacity to generate wealth. Her unwavering mindset, firm like a lighthouse amid a stormy sea, guided me to embrace the same faith decades later.

Our initial step toward cultivating a wealth mindset is shifting our gaze toward abundance. It's an effortless trap to fall into—a scarcity mindset that whispers, "There's never enough." But here's the liberating truth: Our world is a treasure trove, teeming with opportunities just waiting for your touch.

As I reshaped my mindset from scarcity to abundance, I recognized opportunities clad in various disguises. I began to attract positive experiences and circumstances that danced to the rhythm of my newfound belief in abundance. I came to a profound realization that I deserved joy and wealth, as are you. Affirming your worthiness of joy and wealth, you invite the abundance patiently waiting at your doorstep.

Having embraced the abundance mindset, it's now time to crystallize your wildest life and financial goals. What does your heart yearn to achieve? Is it the satisfaction of being debt-free, the security of a retirement fund, the thrill of investing in your dream house, or the anticipation of awe-inspiring vacations? Be audacious and specific about your boundless goals, etch a timeline into them. Once your wildest aspirations are defined, carve a detailed timeline to reach them. This road map keeps you focused, determined, and passionately engaged in actualizing your dreams.

While nursing the bruises of my brain injury, I committed to a goal to regain control over my financial life. I aspired to build wealth that would elevate my life and lay a foundation for future generations. A vision of a future embroidered with financial abundance became my North Star, motivating me toward consistent action. When my mindset morphed, and I realized I wasn't just a mere spectator in a world of abundance and that joy and wealth were my birthrights. Life began to transform. From the negatives emerged a vibrant art collection and a robust investment portfolio. This quantum leap from nothing to something commenced with acknowledging the overflowing wealth around us. Once my mindset shifted, I began to bask in gratitude for what I had, rejoiced in my achievements, and surrounded myself with positivity that reinforced my worthiness of financial abundance.

My journey underlined the significance of diversifying income streams, a safety net against economic uncertainties. Relying solely on one income source is akin to standing on thin ice, vulnerable to unexpected disruptions. Delve into side hustles, freelance work, or investment opportunities to cultivate additional revenue streams. This will not only fortify your financial stability but also unveil a myriad of possibilities, accelerating your journey toward wealth creation.

Amid my recovery, I identified the need to diversify my income, creating multiple avenues for revenue. I breathed life into a small online business, harnessing my skills and passions to generate additional income. This step did more than just reinforce my financial stability—it broadened my mindset, revealing that opportunities for wealth creation are as numerous as the stars, if only we dare to reach for them.

Immerse yourself in a circle of like-minded individuals who echo your financial aspirations. Your social environment profoundly shapes your mindset and habits. Engage with a vibrant community of individuals aimed at building wealth— a haven where you'll find support, encouragement, and valuable advice. You'll inspire each other and stay accountable to your financial goals.

Joining groups and communities of people who shared my vision of financial empowerment was an oasis in my journey. We exchanged strategies, celebrated victories, and offered motivation during challenging times. Being embraced by such individuals reinforced my belief in endless possibilities and gifted me the resilience to persist.

Building wealth is a journey, not a destination. It requires acknowledging the abundance of our world and the realization that with patience and perseverance, this wealth will flow toward you. This transformative journey won't manifest overnight. But armed with dedication and consistency, you can surmount obstacles and setbacks along the path. Embrace these challenges as lessons, adapt your strategies as needed, and remain committed to your vision of financial empowerment, knowing that this world has more than enough.

My journey wasn't smooth sailing. It was a tumultuous ride with setbacks and obstacles threatening to derail my progress. But I refused to let them define me. I learned from my missteps, recalibrated my course when necessary, and clung to the mindset that more money, opportunities, and resources will always flow to me.

By nurturing a wealth mindset and integrating these strategies into your life, you have the power to shatter the chains of financial trauma, bridge the racial wealth gap, and illuminate a brighter future for yourself and your community. Remember, you are the scriptwriter of your financial story. With each stride you take toward financial empowerment, you inspire others to follow in your footsteps.

Seize the abundance waiting for you and embark on this transformative financial empowerment journey. Recall, you have the power to mold your financial destiny, and by nurturing a wealth mindset, you swing open doors to infinite possibilities. Embrace the principles of abundance, crystalize your goals, prioritize financial education, save and invest wisely, eliminate debt, diversify your income, surround yourself with a supportive community, and persist with patience and determination.

The time for change is now. Step into a brighter financial future and set forth on the path to lasting wealth and empowerment. Your journey begins by acknowledging that you deserve joy and wealth, and that there is more than enough to go around. It's time to reach for the stars and claim the prosperity that is rightfully yours.

Breaking News ... You Don't Have to Be Rich to Build Generational Wealth

NOW THAT YOU'RE privy to a fair amount of my life story, I thought I would dispel a widely held fallacy: only the rich can build generational wealth. I, too, was once a firm believer that creating generational wealth was the exclusive prerogative of the affluent or the famous. However, I have since realized that this belief is a mere illusion. The truth is, anyone can cultivate generational wealth by passing down tangible assets like money, real estate, stocks, bonds, and other valuables. But, crucially, this also needs to be paired with a parallel transmission of education and resources to equip the next generation to nurture what they've inherited. Let's be clear, though: Generational poverty can take root when assets are inherited without the vital knowledge or resources needed to foster their growth. Hence, the secret sauce to successful generational wealth creation isn't merely about amassing wealth but also crafting an actionable plan anchored in robust financial education.

To emphasize financial education's crucial role in this journey, allow me to share an episode from my own life, an unfortunate brush with generational poverty. Brace yourself; it's a bit of a face-palm moment. But I share this so you can avoid the pitfalls that I stumbled into.

Looking back, I see how my father's well-intentioned gesture of gifting me an asset—the Dominion Stock—could have laid the foundation for generational wealth. Instead, due to my ignorance, it morphed into a missed opportunity, and a precursor to generational poverty. The asset was great, and additionally, having the financial education alongside it would've been best. I didn't comprehend the asset's true value or how it could be a money tree by growing wealth over time. The education to understand the asset I'd been gifted was absent, and that made all the difference.

Generational wealth encompasses not only the future but also the present. It includes the ability to enjoy life's offerings with loved ones, such as family dinners, vacations, spontaneous road trips, house hunting, or even gathering to strategize and grow as a family. And it is highly connected to ensuring money is growing as the good experiences are happening. Generational wealth is not taking your last dime for a good time. But, using some of your overflow money to do overflow things.

At times we can have overflow money and use it too immaturely because we do not have our cash growing in other areas. One of my most cherished memories of experiencing generational wealth, which was generational poverty, through shared experiences was during my graduation from Howard University. With the funds I received from an insurance claim after a commercial van backed into my new Acura, I could pay for my graduation attire, hair, and a catered party, inviting my loving family to celebrate with me. This experience taught me that wealth transcends material possessions and includes creating memorable experiences and caring for our loved ones, only when a portion of your money is growing and smiling at you. I missed that part because I did not know, even with two degrees at that time (a bachelor's and a master's).

Closing the racial wealth gap and building generational wealth for Black and Brown families, I am reminded that financial security is important for future generations and our parents and grandparents. Financial security allows them to enjoy vacations, good food, and quality time with loved ones if money is growing in other ways. "Never spend your last dime," are words from Renee I live by.

Now that I've learned that building generational wealth is possible for anyone, I'm passionate about sharing my knowledge and experience to help others achieve financial empowerment. In this chapter, I'll share practical steps and action plans that can guide you on your journey to building generational wealth through long-term investing. Please keep in mind this information is for educational purposes only, always do your own research.. Now, that we got that out of the way ...

The first step is to prioritize financial education. It's difficult to invest, save, or manage money without a solid understanding of financial concepts. Educating yourself and your family about financial management and investing at all ages is crucial to building generational wealth. This can involve teaching children about directing their money, the power of compounding interest, and the benefits of long-term investing.

The second step is to establish intergenerational wealth transfer mechanisms. These mechanisms refer to the methods used to pass down wealth from one generation to the next, such as beneficiaries, wills, trusts, and family foundations to name a few. Choosing the right transfer mechanism for your family's unique circumstances is essential. The transfer mechanism should be designed to minimize taxes, avoid disputes among family members, and ensure that the assets are distributed according to the grantor's wishes and how to grow the assets is known by all members of the family.

In addition to financial education and transfer mechanisms, the values and mindset of the family can also play a critical role in building generational wealth. Prioritizing growing money, delayed gratification, and investing for the long term are essential values to instill in future generations.

The family's practice of giving until it hurts can also influence its ability to establish and maintain generational wealth. Engaging in giving back to your family, community, and supporting causes you care about can serve to instill values in future generations and educate them on the importance of giving back, extending beyond monetary contributions. You can share your time, knowledge, experience, prayers, hugs, and various other forms of support. It's important to note that while giving money is beautiful, especially when it is not your last and you have financial growth, your most valuable asset, is your time. Therefore, using your time and resources wisely is crucial, as your generational wealth depends on it.

Finally, building generational wealth is a journey that requires ongoing effort and attention. Educate and mentor future generations to help them maintain and grow what you've built. This can involve everything from teaching them about new investment opportunities to helping them develop a long-term financial plan.

When I became a long-term investor, I understood money growing for the long term no matter how big or small, and teaching the next generation is generational wealth. I truly began to experience generational wealth with my children, aged nine and ten, who already understand investments, building a company, and learning how to grow wealth at their level. They are aware of their college fund via Maryland 529.

They are aware of their investments, savings, and checking accounts via Greenlight. They work to save, invest and spend because we are teaching them that is the way to generational wealth. Although we may not have millions, my children are learning the value of growing wealth in various ways, including embracing our family's rich history of gatherings and togetherness beyond assets and how to build wealth using assets we can do both.

Here are five steps for building generational wealth:

Affirm Your Worthiness of Joy and Wealth: Recognize that you and your family deserve joy and wealth. Affirm and believe in your ability to build generational wealth. Embrace a mindset that allows joy to sustain your journey.

Prioritize Financial Education: Educate yourself and your family about financial concepts, investing, and money management. Teach children about compounding interest, long-term investing, and making informed financial decisions. Continuously expand your financial knowledge.

Establish Mechanisms for Intergenerational Wealth Transfer: Set up mechanisms such as beneficiaries, wills, trusts, or family foundations to facilitate the transfer of wealth across generations. Choose mechanisms that align with your family's circumstances, minimize taxes, prevent disputes, and ensure assets are distributed according to your wishes.

Instill Essential Values and Mindset: Prioritize values that promote wealth growth, delayed gratification, and long-term investment. Teach future generations the importance of financial responsibility, wise financial choices, and the benefits of compound growth. Cultivate a mindset that values asset-building and long-term financial planning.

Practice Philanthropy: Give back to your family, community, and causes you care about. Instill a sense of generosity, social responsibility, and empathy in future generations. Encourage giving beyond monetary contributions, including sharing time, knowledge, experience, and support.

Maintain Ongoing Effort and Mentoring: Building generational wealth is a continuous process. Even after transferring assets, continue to educate and mentor the next generation. Keep them informed about new investment opportunities, assist in developing long-term financial plans, and provide ongoing support as they manage and grow their assets.

By following these steps, you can establish a solid foundation for building generational wealth and ensuring a brighter financial future for yourself, your family, and future generations.

In conclusion, building generational wealth is possible for anyone who is willing to prioritize financial education, establish intergenerational wealth transfer mechanisms, instill essential values and a mindset of delayed gratification, prioritize philanthropy, and approach the journey as an ongoing process of growth and learning. Following these practical steps and action plans can pave the way for a brighter financial future for yourself, your family, and future generations.

Balancing Financial Styles in a Relationship

*P*ICTURE THIS: YOUR journey to financial freedom is well underway, your investment portfolio is blossoming, and your dreams of building generational wealth are gradually coming into focus. All is going according to plan … until an unexpected roadblock appears on the horizon: your better half. Now, don't get me wrong. I adore my partner more than anything. She's my rock, my confidante, and my compass in the storms of life. But when it comes to money, let's just say we're more like Batman and the Joker than Batman and Robin.

My wife subscribes to the philosophy of dispatching bills with the speed of a Marvel superhero, while I tend to be more like a Zen gardener, tending to our money and nurturing it to grow. Let's just say, it's sparked more heated debates than a presidential election.

You've heard the adage, "opposites attract," right? In our case, it's less about attraction and more about a battle of financial wills. My wife prefers to take the safe route, clutching her purse strings tighter than a drum. On the other hand, I like to dance on the edge of the financial dance floor, taking calculated risks that could lead to bigger paydays.

So, how do two people with such disparate financial views share a life—and a bank account—without constant conflict? Divide and conquer, my friends! In our money matters, we've learned to lean into our strengths. She's the Bill Slayer, vanquishing debts left and right with superhero zeal. And me?

I'm the growth guru, meticulously scouting for investment opportunities to fatten our nest egg.

It's our personal financial yin and yang, a balance that allows us to cover all bases effectively. And while we may not see eye to eye on every dollar and cent, we're positive proof that even financial opposites can find common ground when it comes to building a secure future together.

However, during times when money is tight, I've learned that it's important not to overwhelm her with the full financial picture. My wife's capacity for handling financial stress isn't as strong as mine, so I make an effort to shield her from unnecessary anxiety. This doesn't mean I'm hiding important information from her, but rather, I'm providing her with the details she needs to know without causing undue stress.

The key to navigating these differences in financial style is understanding and respecting each other's perspectives. It's important to acknowledge that there's no one-size-fits-all approach to money management. If we're working together toward a common goal of financial stability and generational wealth, we can find a balance that suits both our styles.

Navigating differences in financial styles can be challenging, but it's an essential part of building a strong relationship. My advice to others facing similar challenges is to recognize and appreciate each other's financial styles. Embrace the differences, divide responsibilities based on your strengths, and most importantly, communicate openly and honestly about your goals and concerns.

My wife and I are still working on perfecting this balance in our financial life. We've made progress, but problems still arise, and life continues. It's important to remember that growth is an ongoing process, and we must be patient with ourselves and each other as we work toward our shared goals.

Do not be afraid of differences and the tension that may arise when your visions for your financial future don't align perfectly. This tension can catalyze growth and understanding, as it forces you to communicate and find common ground. By embracing these differences and working through them together, you can create a harmonious financial life built on trust, understanding, and a shared vision for the future.

Ultimately, the key to successfully navigating financial differences is to keep the lines of communication open, be willing to compromise, and always strive for growth, both individually and as a couple. As you face challenges together, you'll learn more about each other's strengths and weaknesses, and ultimately, you'll become a stronger, more united team working toward a brighter financial future.

The Building Blocks of Investing: The Top 15 Terms You Need to Know

*I*NVESTING CAN FEEL overwhelming, especially if you're just starting out. However, it's important to remember that you can learn and grow as an investor. Don't allow the learning curve to make you quit before you begin. You can do it. If I can do it with a damaged brain and no money, I know you can do it, too. To be a successful long-term investor, it's important to understand the building blocks of investing.

This includes terms like *long-term investing*, *stocks*, *bonds*, *mutual funds*, *brokerage account*, *unrealized gains*, *unrealized loss*, and *compound interest*. By understanding these concepts, you'll be on your way to becoming a successful investor.

Well, folks, I see we've reached the point where I bring out my financial dictionary. Trust me, you're going to want to save this list. It's the decoder ring you need to crack the code of the finance world!

Asset: Picture an asset like a golden goose. It's something valuable you own, like a car, house, money, or stock, and it can lay golden eggs to make you more money over time.

Diversification: Think of diversification as a financial buffet. You don't want to pile your plate with just one dish, right? Instead, you spread your investments over different asset types, so if one flops, the others could still make your investment belly happy.

Dividend: Imagine your favorite company throwing a pizza party and sharing slices with everyone who owns a piece of it. That's essentially a dividend—a share of the profits!

Portfolio: Your portfolio is like your prized stamp collection. It's a collection of all the different investments you've made.

Risk tolerance: This one's a bit like spicy food. Some folks can handle the heat (risk), while others prefer a milder dish. Risk tolerance is about how much you can stomach the value of your investments going up and down.

Stock: When you buy a stock, you get a tiny slice of a company. Like owning a piece of a pizza pie.

Bond: Picture lending your friend money; they promise to pay you back with some interest. That's what a bond is, but your friend happens to be a company or the government.

Mutual fund: It's like a giant pot of financial stew. Everyone chips in, and the money is used to buy a mix of investments.

ETF (Exchange-traded fund): It's like a sibling of mutual funds. But unlike its brother, it can be bought and sold like a stock. It's still a big group of different investments, though.

Capital gains: The joy of selling an investment for more than you paid for it. It's like buying a bike for $100 and selling it for $200. Ka-ching!

Capital losses: The opposite of capital gains. It's the "ouch" moment when you sell an investment for less than you bought it for.

Index: It's like a measuring stick for a specific group of companies. It helps you compare the performance of your investments to others.

Market capitalization: This is how we size up a company. It's the total value based on its stock price and how many shares it has.

Compound interest: Remember the snowball effect? Your earnings start earning too, and your money pile gets bigger over time.

Dollar-cost averaging: It's like shopping regularly for your investments. You invest the same amount regularly, regardless of the price. It's like buying your favorite ice cream every week, whether it's on sale or full price.

Long-term investing is like the slow cooker of wealth creation. It takes time, but the flavors are worth the wait!

Short-term investing: It's like a hot potato. Quick moves, often buying and selling within a year or less. Not my cup of tea, though. I'd rather sip my investments slowly and savor the flavor over time!

Phew! Well, that's our crash course in Investing 101. Stick with me, and soon you'll be throwing around these terms like a Wall Street veteran!

Investing $100 – A Step-by-Step Guide

"The content provided by Ruby 'SunShine' Taylor is intended for educational purposes only and should not be considered as personalized financial advice."

 ET READY FOR a wild ride because you're about to join the thrilling world of stock market investing! Yes, you read that right. Even if your bank account looks more like a kiddie pool than an ocean, with as little as $100 or less, you can dip your toes into investing. It's like learning to swim—it doesn't matter how deep the pool is; it's all about making that initial splash!

Step 1: Meet your new BFFs – brokerage firms!

Choosing a brokerage firm is like auditioning contestants for a dating show. You want someone reliable, respected, and with a good track record. Your contestants? Fidelity, Vanguard,

Charles Schwab, TD Ameritrade, E*TRADE, Robinhood, Acorns, or Stash. It's like *The Bachelorette*, but for your money!

Step 2: Choose your money's playground

You have two playgrounds to let your money frolic in: retirement accounts (think: IRA) and personal accounts (the flexible ones!). Retirement accounts come with tax benefits, while personal ones let your money play around a bit more freely. Pick what suits you and your financial goals best.

Step 3: Sign up for an account

Next, take your chosen brokerage firm on a date. Visit their website, open an account, and make it "Facebook official." They'll ask some personal and investment-related questions —don't worry; it's not an interrogation, just a way for them to recommend the best investments for you.

Step 4: Fill Your account's tummy

It's time to feed your new account. Most firms accept electronic transfers or checks. Make sure you've got enough to meet any minimum investment requirements—even your account doesn't like to go hungry!

Step 5: Let the knowledge floodgates open

Next, you'll want to transform into a financial Sherlock Holmes. Dive into resources like FinancialJoySchool.com, Motley Fool, and Morningstar to get a grip on stocks, bonds, mutual funds, and ETFs. Remember, knowledge is power!

Step 6: Become an investment Picasso

Now, it's time to paint your investment masterpiece. Distribute your $100 across different assets, like index funds, investment platforms, or individual stocks. You're the Picasso of your financial destiny.

Step 7: Join the investing marathon

Here's where the rubber meets the road. You start with your $100 and keep investing consistently every month. Run the marathon, not the sprint.

Let me give you a glimpse of the finish line. If you consistently invest $100 every month, with an 11 percent average interest rate (which is slightly less than the S&P 500's return since 2012), here's how it could look:

10 years: $20,350.35
20 years: $77,849.63
30 years: $241,114.28
50 years: $2,020,981.87

Just remember, it's like predicting the weather—estimates may vary!

Step 8: Place your orders

Ready to make your investment purchases? Use the brokerage firm's online platform or call your broker if you want to go old school. Review your orders carefully—always check the receipt!

Step 9: Watch your garden grow

Keep an eye on your investments. Check in on your financial "plants" regularly, but don't panic when the wind blows a bit. Remember, you're growing a forest, not only a single tree.

Step 10: Reinvest your earnings

When your investments start to bear fruit in the form of dividends or capital gains, plant those seeds right back in! It's like making your money do the salsa—the dance of compound growth!

Step 11: The two p's – patience and persistence

Finally, investing is a marathon, not a sprint. Stay patient, persistent, and keep your eye on the prize. You're aiming for the magical number—your financial goal.

Stay informed, keep learning, and be ready to adapt your strategy. As you grow more comfortable, consider feeding your investments a bit more than $100. Your initial plunge into the investment pool may be with $100, but with consistency and focus, you can turn that kiddie pool into an ocean of wealth.

Remember, investing isn't about getting rich quick—it's about creating opportunities for yourself and your loved ones. It's about transforming that $100 into a key to your financial freedom. So, let's get started! It's time to make a splash!

Crafting Our Legacy: Building Generational Wealth

*T*HE DOWN-HOME SMELL of fresh wood burning in an iron stove my grandparent's house in North Carolina will forever be a reminder that home ownership matters. Big or small, every home has its own story and set of challenges to overcome. Like many Black and Brown families, my grandparents weren't handed a golden ticket of generational wealth. Instead, they faced the uphill task of building their legacy, starting from scratch.

Now, let's dig into a little family history. My grandma's family, back in the late 1800s, owned their land, farmed their crops, and built a life from the soil up. They were a step ahead of my grandpa's family, and love was the bridge that connected these two different worlds. This love story wasn't without its hiccups though—like when my grandmother chose to marry a sharecropper, a decision that didn't sit well with her folks.

Grandpa was a simple man. He found contentment working on someone else's land, while Grandma had a different dream. She knew what ownership felt like, and she yearned for that sense of security and freedom. After years of persuasion, Grandpa finally saw the light. He bought land, built a home, and even managed to squeeze in a small farm in the backyard. Money was still tight, but the land was spacious enough for my aunt and uncle to build their home and raise their family.

Why am I spinning this tale, you may ask? Well, it's because knowledge is power. Grandma knew the comfort and security of ownership, which Grandpa was initially oblivious to. Her knowledge and persistence led to them buying their own piece of land, a decision that gave their eleven children a place to always call home. And that, my friends, is what generational wealth is all about.

Her relentless advocacy bore fruit, as my grandfather eventually yielded to her vision. The plot of land he procured along with a modest house and a backyard might have strained their finances, yet it was expansive enough for my aunt and uncle to lay the foundations of their homes. Thus, two among the eleven children were provided a substantial leap and all eleven children had access to land of their own, which gave them a place to always call home. This microcosm of generational wealth may appear insignificant, but the ramifications were profound in the grand scheme of life.

Indeed, while real estate acquisition is an essential cornerstone of wealth building, I'd be remiss not to emphasize the stock market's critical role in this endeavor. Imagine our wealth-building strategy as a building under construction. Real estate forms the robust foundation, while the stock market constitutes the bricks and mortar, and shapes our wealth structure.

Moreover, the advent of digital trading platforms and the democratization of investment knowledge have broken down the barriers to entry into the stock market. Today, anyone can invest in the market with a few clicks on their smartphone, making this wealth-building tool accessible to all.

Real estate and stock market investments are two sides of the same coin, each complementing and reinforcing the other. While real estate provides tangible assets, a steady income stream, and significant tax benefits, stock market investments offer unparalleled liquidity, flexibility, tax benefits, and potential for exponential growth.

The wealth transferred through generations via the stock market is an untapped gold mine for our community. Imagine what we can accomplish as a collective if we could harness this potential for our families?

My *Why*

If my family legacy was not enough motivation behind my mission reading this shocking fact pushed me into action—according to the report "The Road to Zero Wealth" from the Institute of Policy Studies, by 2053, White median net worth will be $137,000, while Black and Latino wealth will drop to a staggering $0. This glaring disparity lit a fire in me to make a difference to change this narrative.

Our journey began small, teaching my cousin about investing. Seeing the spark in his eyes, I knew I was onto something. I wanted to create a space where my community could learn about long-term investing, where they automatically felt welcome and didn't have to dust off their feet before stepping in. This led me to create the Legacy! Card Game. It's a fun, jargon-free game that teaches Black and Brown families how to build generational wealth.

Uplifted by the success of the card game, I started the Financial Joy School, a digital platform dedicated to making investing fun for Black and Brown families. We offer free resources like videos, infographics, and calculators to help our community better understand the financial world.

The journey isn't over, though. There's more work to be done. I want to create more resources and games and integrate them into schools and community organizations. I'm dreaming of becoming the NerdWallet for the Black and Brown community, offering unbiased financial advice to help close the racial wealth gap.

This journey isn't a walk in the park. Building a legacy is a tough task, full of setbacks and obstacles. But it's in these challenges that I find my determination growing stronger, my resolve steelier and I feel the resilience of my grandmother pushing my grandfather into action. When I look around and see Black and Brown families who've used the Legacy! Card Game and the Financial Joy School to build their generational wealth, I can imagine how my grandmother felt moving into her home. My community success stories fuel my passion and push me to keep going and doing more.

My ultimate vision? To foster financial empowerment and generational wealth for Black and Brown families and all marginalized communities. We must break the poverty cycle and create a brighter future for ourselves and our communities. I extend an open invitation to everyone to join me on this journey. Let's make a pledge to strive for financial empowerment and generational wealth.

Picture a tree, deeply rooted in the fertile soil of knowledge and financial wisdom, with branches reaching out to embrace generations of Black and Brown families. This tree represents the legacy that I've dedicated my life to building—a legacy of financial empowerment and generational wealth for marginalized communities especially Black and Brown families.

Just think about it, if my grandparents could create such a legacy, what can we, as a community, achieve when we tap into the wealth-building potential of the stock market and real estate?

Protecting Your Legacy: Why You Need a Will and Living Trust

*H*AVE YOU EVER thought about what will happen to your assets once you're gone? It's not something we like to think about, but it's essential to have a plan in place to protect your hard-earned wealth and ensure that it's passed down to your loved ones or directed where you want it to go. With all the hard work and struggles that we face in life, it's important to think about the future.

You might think you don't need a will or a living trust because you don't have much, but that's not true. You need a will if you have a retirement fund, savings or checking account, a car, or anything of value. You don't have to be rich to need a will and living trust. It's never too early to start planning for the future, but it can be too late.

Many people, including some of the most well-known celebrities, did not have a will or living trust when they passed away. Aretha Franklin, Chadwick Boseman, Martin Luther King Jr., Billie Holiday, Prince, Abraham Lincoln, Bob Marley,

Tupac, Amy Winehouse, and Michael Jackson are just a few examples. Not having a plan in place for their assets caused problems for their families and loved ones, and their legacies were not fully protected.

So, let's break down what a will and living trust is:

A will is a legal document that outlines your wishes to distribute your assets after you die. While a will is better than nothing, it's often not enough to protect your heirs from taxes, creditors, and other legal issues that can arise after your death.

A living trust, on the other hand, is a legal document that holds your assets during your lifetime and can continue to hold them after you pass away. It's a more comprehensive way to protect your assets and ensure they're distributed according to your wishes.

Sadly, too many families spend a lot of money on lawyers and time in probate court to get what is rightfully theirs, all because the family didn't have a will and living trust. That's why ensuring you have both to safeguard your hard-earned wealth and protect your heirs is crucial.

I remember a conversation with my mother when I advised her that she and my father needed more than a will; they needed a living trust. Her response was, "When I die, I won't be worrying about none of that stuff." But, the truth is we will. That's why I'm screaming from the rooftops, don't throw away your assets by not having a will and living trust.

I understand that hiring an estate lawyer can be expensive and out of reach for many people. But the good news is that there are tech companies out there that are making estate planning accessible and affordable for the average person. One such company is Trust & Will. For just $159, you can get a will; for $599, you can get a living trust. They even offer payment plans to make it easier for everyone to protect their families and assets.

Of course, if you need more assistance and would like an estate planner, you can always turn to the Association of Black Estate Planning Professionals (ABEPP). They have a network of professionals who can help you create a comprehensive plan to protect your assets and ensure your wishes are fulfilled.

Don't make the mistake of thinking that you don't need a will or living trust. By creating a plan, you'll be protecting your hard-earned wealth and providing for your loved ones for years to come. Protecting your legacy and ensuring that your assets are passed down as you intended is important.

Creating a will and living trust also provides comfort and peace of mind, knowing that your wishes will be fulfilled and your loved ones will be cared for after you pass away. Not having a plan in place can leave your family in a difficult and stressful situation during an already emotionally challenging time.

In addition to outlining your wishes for the distribution of your assets, a will also serves as a guiding document for who will oversee making medical decisions for you and what you would like to happen after you transition. These decisions may be left up to the court without a will, and your wishes may not be known or followed.

It's important to note that estate planning isn't just for older adults. Young adults should also consider creating a will and living trust, especially if they have children or other dependents. Unexpected events can happen, and having a plan in place can ensure that their loved ones are taken care of and their assets are protected.

A will and living trust are crucial for protecting your legacy and ensuring that your hard-earned assets are distributed according to your wishes. It's never too early to start planning for the future, but it can be too late. By taking the time to create a plan, you'll be protecting your loved ones and providing for them for years to come. Don't let your assets go to waste by not having a will and living trust. Invest in your future and your legacy by creating a plan today.

Here's a simple breakdown to get you started:

Start with a will: Even if you don't think you have significant assets, start with a will. It should name the executor, the person who will handle your estate, and guardians for any minor children. It's an essential document that everyone should have.

Consider a living trust: A living trust allows your assets to pass to your beneficiaries without going through probate, which can be a long and costly process. It's also private, unlike a will, which becomes a matter of public record.

Power of attorney: Assign someone to make financial decisions on your behalf if you cannot do so. This person will handle your financial affairs and ensure your bills are paid, and your financial obligations are met.

Health-care directive: This document specifies what medical treatments you would or would not want at the end of life and names a person (your health-care proxy) who will make sure your health-care providers follow your wishes.

Beneficiary designations: Ensure that you have updated beneficiaries on all your financial accounts, including retirement accounts and life insurance policies. These designations bypass a will, so keeping them current is important.

Digital assets: With our lives increasingly online, it's important to consider your digital assets. This includes everything from online banking and investment accounts to social media profiles and digital photos. Choose a digital executor who will handle these assets according to your wishes. Estate planning is an ongoing process and should be revisited at regular intervals and after major life events like a marriage, divorce, birth of a child, or death in the family. It may seem complex and overwhelming, but with the right guidance, it doesn't have to be. Don't leave your family guessing about your intentions and struggling to sort out your affairs after you're gone. Take control now, plan for the future, and build a legacy that you and your loved ones can be proud of.

Remember, it's not just about protecting your assets; it's about caring for your loved ones and preserving your legacy.

So, start planning today. Your assets are your legacy even if you think you don't have much. Protect them, and ensure they go where you want them to go. That's what estate planning is all about.

INTERMISSION

Rising Above Hardship with Faith and Love – My Mother's Story

Written by Arline Taylor

*M*Y NAME IS Arline Taylor, and I am the mother of Ruby "SunShine" Taylor. I want to share how I rose above difficulties fueled by faith and love. These two pillars have guided me through the darkest moments and lifted me to new heights.

Slavery had a lasting impact on my people; some of my children still carry the weight of that horrific history. They feel trapped, believing they can never rise above their circumstances. Slavery did a number on many of us, instilling a belief that we can never succeed and will always be beneath others. But I am grateful for the children who haven't succumbed to that mindset. They still believe in their ability to overcome and create a better life for themselves. My daughter (the author of the book *Sunshine*) knows there is more to life than what we've experienced. She radiates hope and determination; I am confident she will reach every goal and dream her heart desires.

I'd like to share how Ruby Sunshine came into my life and earned her special name. I had a rough time just getting her here. The pregnancy was difficult, and the doctor wanted me to choose her life or mine. I chose her life, and my God was able to deliver us both from the medical crisis. Glory be to God. So, she had a rough time coming up. But Ruby Sunshine is here. And one day, I asked the Lord, I said, "She had such a hard time, Lord. What should she be to me?" And God answered, "Sunshine." Until this day, Ruby's sunshine will always be to me.

Having Ruby Sunshine wasn't my first hardship. Throughout my life, racism and the legacy of slavery have played a significant role in my hardship. Growing up on a farm as a sharecropper in North Carolina was a struggle that seemed to never end. They heavily burdened me and my family and sometimes filled me with anger and hatred. But Jesus taught me to let go of that hatred because they couldn't stop me. They tried, but they couldn't break my spirit. The memories of backbreaking work, mistreatment, and discrimination constantly reminded us of our challenges. But throughout it all, my unwavering belief in Christ gave me the strength to keep going. I knew I could overcome any obstacle if I had faith.

One aspect of racism and the historical discrimination of Jim Crow that affected me deeply was the unfair wages we received. They never paid us what we truly deserved. I fought for fair pay, but they always denied me. Yet, I found ways to survive and make the most out of what little I had. I stretched every dollar and used my resourcefulness to provide for my family. Even though they tried to keep me down, I refused to let them define my worth. I knew my worth came from God, and I relied on him to sustain me. So, I prayed to God and asked him to help me find a way out of that place in North Carolina.

And somehow, someway, Jesus answered my prayers. He guided me to New York, using a newspaper ad looking for domestic workers, and that gave me a one-way ticket to a fresh start. It was a blessing beyond measure. I arrived in the city and took on odd jobs, working day and night to make ends meet. As I grew older, the financial game became more challenging. Through those jobs, God showed me a path to escape the weight of debt that had burdened me for so long. I worked tirelessly, climbing my way up step by step, with God's blessings and grace guiding me. Jesus showed me how to overcome my limitations and rise above the hardships that threatened to hold me back. I was determined to care for my children and provide for my family.

Since my husband and I had to feed our children, I took whatever work I could find, even if it meant being underpaid. A former boss would often say, "Don't give away your hard work for nothing, as he paid me better than most, yet he still underpaid me too. He would say, "Go where they pay you what you deserve." But I knew that if I went into a house to clean, I could make it look brand new by the end of the day. I worked tirelessly, cooking for their families and serving them. I made do with what I had, turning a little into a lot. I stretched a dollar and turned it into ten, twenty, then a hundred. I persevered through adversity and didn't let my struggles go to waste. I trusted God to bless every job opportunity and provide for myself and my children.

Despite the hardships, my children brought immense joy into my life. They were the sunshine that brightened my darkest days. I wanted to give them a better life, free from the struggles I faced. I wanted them to grow up knowing their worth and believing in themselves. The struggles I endured shaped my perspective on life. I didn't let slavery define me, nor did wisdom and knowledge come from that dark chapter of history. They came from the Creator, from God himself.

Slavery impacted some of my children terribly, but I refuse to let them go through what I experienced. I have always been there for them, supporting them so they wouldn't fall. Sometimes, I wonder if spoiling them hindered their growth. Maybe if I had let them face their struggles, they would have grown more. But I couldn't bear to see them fall because I had dropped too many times myself.

It was one of the worst things I've experienced when my daughter got hurt. I couldn't believe something so terrible could happen to her. But I trusted God to take care of her. People didn't understand when I cooked all kinds of food and left a full plate for her, untouched, while she rested. They thought I was crazy, suggesting I get a hotel and stay nearby. But I knew she was OK because I had placed her in God's hands. He blessed her with wonderful friends, lawyers, and others who cared for her. I had faith in God's plan for her, and all I wanted was for her to rest, heal, and feel loved.

Through the rough times, I relied on prayer and the grace of God to overcome. There were moments when I cried more than I prayed, my tears flowing like a river. But God always dried them up, giving me the strength to carry on. I looked upon my children, knowing I could make this journey because God was by my side. He never left me, even in the toughest times.

Even today, I still eat the leftovers my children leave behind, just as I did when they were young. It's a reminder of where we came from and the hardships we endured. But now, my children can eat whatever they want, experiencing the abundance that was once beyond our reach. They can enjoy chicken and even raw steak if they desire. They can taste the flavors of the rich, despite our humble beginnings. I excelled because God made a way where there seemed to be no way.

I cultivated my own garden in New York, growing collard greens, tomatoes, and cucumbers. I became skilled in preserving and canning food. My house has been free of hunger for over sixty years because I trust in God. He taught me how to kill and prepare animals, ensuring we always had enough to eat. Even to this day, we eat well, thanks to the provisions of the Almighty.

Jesus is the source of my resilience. He blows through the wind, unseen yet mighty. Like the wind, he is there, guiding, providing, and lifting us up. I know this because I have felt his presence within me. Through Jesus, I have overcome the hardships of my past and continue to face each day with hope and unwavering faith.

I want you, dear reader, to understand the power of Jesus in my life. He is the reason I have triumphed over adversity. He is the reason I have been able to provide for my children and give them a better life. Jesus is my constant companion, my rock, and my salvation.

As you embark on your journey, remember that Jesus is with you, too. Trust in him even when times are tough, and it feels like there is no way forward. He will guide you, strengthen you, and give you the resilience to overcome any obstacle. Jesus is the trustworthy source of hope and the ultimate provider.

May my story inspire you to hold on to faith (whatever you believe), to believe in the unseen, and to excel against all odds. And when you face hardships, remember that you can find the strength to rise above through prayer and grace. I believe with Jesus by your side, you can make it, just as I have.

I am a testament to the resilience and power of faith. May you find the same in your own life. God bless you on your journey, and may his love and grace carry you through all the days to come.

Embracing Change and Finding Purpose

Written by Chantel Roche

As a Latina of diverse heritage, born to a Guatemalan mother and an Italian-American father, my cultural roots extend across continents, weaving a rich tapestry of varied traditions and perspectives. This intricate blend of cultures has proven to be fertile soil for self-exploration and curiosity, allowing me to appreciate the dynamism of my identity and connect with individuals from a broad array of backgrounds.

My parents drew a clear course for my life during my early years: a path leading toward law. The notions embedded in me since childhood were that education was a privilege to be cherished and that a law career epitomized achievement. Consequently, these influences steered me toward law school, a direction fueled not by innate passion but by a perceived absence of alternatives.

Throughout my upbringing, my parents' expectations served as a guiding blueprint for my future. Their persistent emphasis on education as the ultimate advantage—a powerful tool for protection and empowerment—was instilled within me since childhood. To them, the pinnacle of success was embodied in their daughter's pursuit of a law career. For a significant portion of my life, this trajectory appeared unchangeable.

Often, I was referred to as "bossy," a characteristic they considered ideal for a future lawyer. Because I struggled in math, fields like science and medicine, according to their belief, would take me too long to catch up and I would be better off focusing on my strengths. Creative fields were also not encouraged as there was "no money" in art. As a result, my fate seemed predetermined. Becoming anything other than a lawyer was neither considered nor endorsed. Thus, I found myself in the field of law—not driven by desire but constrained by a desire to please my parents and not having a moment to consider other possibilities.

Despite their strict aspirations, my parents imparted a potent belief: "Education can never harm you, only benefit you." Inspired by this mantra, I began to perceive education as a stepping stone. I enjoyed college to the fullest, pursuing a bachelor of arts from Arizona State University in Spanish. My degree further connected me to my roots as I had forgotten my Spanish in order to assimilate into public school. In addition to my BA, I earned a certificate in Latin American studies and studied abroad in both Spain and Italy. I went directly to Roger Williams School of Law after graduating from Arizona State University. While I gave law school a chance, I knew that the practice of law was not going to be for me. Despite this and by pure grit and determination I graduated from law school on time—leaving with a set of analytical skills and deep knowledge of the pitfalls of our legal system.

However, it was a friend in law school who put me on my ultimate path to diversity, equity and inclusion (DEI) work. This friend saw potential in me that I didn't and recommended that I become a program coordinator for a not-for-profit, helping underserved and underrepresented youth get into college. I was doing "DEI work" before it was known as the field that it is today. While I only spent two years with the program, it left a mark on me that I did not know I would return to.

In the years that followed, I discovered my vast potential and grew both personally and professionally by saying yes to a variety of opportunities. I worked in many industries including higher education, television, and real estate. Ten years after graduating from law school, I was at a crossroads. Prompted by a move to Massachusetts and not knowing what my next step would be, I opted to take the Massachusetts bar exam. Relying on the mantra that education, or in this case a credential, can never hurt, I sat and passed the bar.

One would think my story would end there, happily practicing law and "coming home". However, this was not the case. Sitting for this exam gave me time to think about what I wanted to do with my life. When I wasn't studying, I was looking at various opportunities, truly looking at my skills and trying to match them with an industry, a cause, something to gravitate toward. My mind constantly went back to my not-for-profit experience and I homed in on my love of helping people become the best versions of themselves. Soon after, I saw an opportunity with the United States Tennis Association of New England for a diversity and inclusion manager position. I could not have been more thrilled with the job description—finally something that combined my love of helping people mixed with social justice! Something I could not see myself doing in law school suddenly became a reality when I interviewed and ultimately got the position.

This was my true career homecoming and I immersed myself in all things diversity, equity and inclusion.

The concept of fostering environments where differences are celebrated resonated deeply within me. Concurrently, my career shift aligned with a global swing toward these values, catalyzed by the murder of George Floyd. This incident galvanized organizations globally to prioritize equality and confront systemic biases.

Now, as a diversity, equity and inclusion director at Staples, I am committed to dismantling systemic prejudices and nurturing an inclusive atmosphere. My path, from a law-oriented childhood to becoming a leader in diversity and inclusion, has not been linear but it has been profoundly enlightening. The experiences I've undergone, both the triumphs and trials, have sculpted the person I am today, instilling in me resilience, empathy, and the vitality of welcoming change.

Throughout this journey, I've learned that education transcends traditional boundaries. My law degree did not limit me to a legal career; it served as a gateway to my true calling. The skills I honed—critical thinking, comprehension of societal structures and law, and navigating intricate situations—have been invaluable in my current role.

In retrospect, I appreciate the challenges and lessons from my early journey of being confined by familial expectations and having the privilege and freedom to reimagine and reshape that confinement. These experiences have taught me that while our past shapes us, it does not confine us. It was through self-exploration and determination that I arrived at my true calling. My journey is a testament to the transformative power of education, the value of self-discovery, and the impact of embracing diversity and inclusion.

As I forge ahead, my commitment is unwavering: to create a world where everyone's unique contributions are recognized, and they can thrive in an environment of inclusivity and respect. Despite uncertainties, I remain confident in the skills I've honed, the knowledge I've accrued, and the resilience I've developed.

My journey speaks to the power of education, the necessity of self-discovery, and the profound effect of embracing diversity, equity and inclusivity. It's about challenging societal norms and carving your own unique path. Most importantly, it highlights the importance of resilience and the courage required to follow your passions, even when they defy conventional wisdom.

My journey is an ongoing adventure, full of excitement and endless possibilities. I am eager to embrace the future and the continued impact I can have. With each step I take, my determination grows stronger, fueling my passion to empower others to seize control of their financial lives. Together, we can shatter barriers, challenge norms, and forge a brighter, more inclusive financial future for all. The journey ahead is promising, and I am committed to creating lasting change and leaving a powerful legacy of financial empowerment.

Charting a New Course: Navigating the Finance Industry

Written by Tomeka Brown, CFP®, CFEI

F I HAD to recall a defining moment in my life that shaped my perspective on finances, it would have to be as a young girl in the Girl Scouts. It was my week to bring in snacks for the rest of the troop. So, my dad took me to the store, and I distinctly remember him picking up a pack of thin butter cookies. And I thought to myself, "Is that it?" The other girls always bought elaborate spreads when it was their time to bring snacks and here, I was unsure if we would even have enough to share with everyone. We walked to the counter, and he pulled out a pocketful of change. He had been in a motorcycle accident shortly before and his hand was still healing so he asked me to count out the coins for the young lady at the register. To this day I don't know if my dad was just being cheap, if he was being resourceful by using the coins he had saved, or if that was really all he had to spare at that given moment, but I remember saying … if I can help it, I don't ever want to be in a place where I HAVE to count coins. Nor did I want my children to ever feel embarrassed (whether intentionally or unintentionally) that I as their parent couldn't provide. In hindsight I understand that wasn't our case at all. I realize that my family was not poor in any way … we traveled extensively as children, had dirt bikes, and go-karts, and truly never wanted for anything. However, that moment has always stuck out for me as a defining moment where even as a child I started to think differently about finances.

While I didn't know how that needed to translate at such a young age, I began to think in a very linear way. I knew I needed to get good grades in high school to get a scholarship to pay for college. Then I needed good grades in undergrad to get into grad school. Then the master's I obtained would secure the high-paying career, thus providing financial freedom. While I never asked, I didn't think my family could afford to pay for me to go to college, so I wanted to pave my own way. And I did just that … laser focused with every step.

During my undergraduate years at Drexel University, I found my true direction. I participated in a five-year co-op program that allowed me to rotate into various corporate positions. My first real job with real benefits. They discussed topics like preparing for retirement and investment vehicles such as 401(k)s and it was all so new to me. I realized there was this new realm of financial knowledge that I knew nothing about, but I knew I needed to absorb as much as possible to catch up for lost time. I began researching financial topics online and printing out pages to create a binder. There was no real organization … just loose pages and handwritten notes. Then I would study whatever I added to the binder, show it to my friends, and ask them if they knew about these concepts. I can confidently say over 90 percent of them didn't. So, I would share my binder with them and talk them through what I was learning during breaks, in the cafeteria, in between classes, when and wherever. I realized there was so much more to finances than having a checking and savings account. My self-made binder was becoming my financial guide and the birth of my passion for teaching financial literacy. I discovered that I had the ability to digest intricate financial ideas and jargon and then explain it in simplified terms so that they could understand it. I remember their "aha" moments bringing me joy.

I abandoned the idea of international business and marketing and pursued specialized studies and a career in the financial services industry. I started out as an associate to learn the field, and then embarked on my journey as a wealth manager. I learned a lot in my years in the role across various firms, but the most important lesson learned was the fact that you will burn out quickly if you don't love what you do. I loved advising, but not as much as I just loved educating. I didn't care if you had $1 or $1 million dollars, I was in my element when I could teach you something to better your financial situation and reach your goals. That didn't always align with the respective firms' goals of bringing in assets. Once I acknowledged that gathering assets was no longer my personal career goal or priority, I began to look for an opportunity that would allow me to keep my credentials but in a slightly different capacity.

Being a young, Black, woman in the financial services industry presented its own challenges. Who I was by nature presented what appeared to be three strikes against me. The industry was dominated by older, White, men. I faced blatant bias and stereotypes from clients who questioned my competence based on my age, and internally I faced inequalities compared to my counterparts with no real explanation, even though in many cases I had more credentials. So, again I had to shift my mentality. The degrees were no longer enough. I pursued further studies to obtain the highest regard as a financial planner. My Certified Financial Planning designation was necessary to level the playing field for me. I found that I had to adorn my walls with my certifications to get some clients comfortably through my office doors. But once I began talking, if there was any concern before, it appeared to evaporate. I enjoyed building relationships with my clients based on trust, empathy, and understanding. Without fail, it continued to be my desire to educate my clients that distinguished me from others.

My journey led me to my current role as the manager of training for a financial group. I created a comprehensive training program and now lead a team of trainers who educate new financial advisors to the firm. This position has brought me immense satisfaction and renewed energy. I can stay connected to the industry while learning a new skill set and emphasizing general education and community involvement. However, transitioning to this role wasn't without its challenges either. I initially took a pay cut and had to navigate dual responsibilities before settling into my role. But the peace I had was worth it.

When reflecting on your journey thus far in life, you must consider the personal successes and failures that got you where you are today. I believe graduating from college and purchasing my home as significant personal successes.

Graduating was a groundbreaking achievement, as I was the first in my family to earn a graduate degree. Buying a home was another milestone, a physical representation of sacrifice, planning, and God. It symbolized a step toward building generational wealth and financial stability.

Amid my successes, I've also faced failures and learned valuable lessons along the way. Most notably, learning some of the unspoken "rules" of corporate, private sector America. While you should never quiet who you are as a person, just be cognizant of how you are perceived. Being outspoken as a young Black woman in corporate America didn't always work in my favor. You hear about the "angry Black woman" label, but it takes on a different meaning when you're stigmatized as such for having a voice, an opinion, an identity, or difference of opinion. To this day, I am still learning to navigate the corporate world, but I'm able to leverage my unique perspective as a young Black woman to bring fresh insights and ideas to the table.

I believe it starts with education and awareness when it comes to encouraging more Black women to pursue careers in finance. Many individuals may not consider finance as a viable career path due to limited exposure or preconceived notions. By sharing my story and educating I hope to inspire young

Black women to explore this field and provide them with the necessary knowledge to succeed. Mentors are valuable. I didn't have a formal mentor, but oddly enough, an older White man I worked with during my first position after college took me under his wing, shared his insights, and guided me indirectly into my career path. It shows how you never know who or how someone may impact your life. Therefore, always make yourself available as a resource to others as you never know how you may impact someone's life.

Throughout my journey, I learned the importance of perseverance, self-education, and embracing opportunities. While my career took a different trajectory than I initially envisioned, I couldn't be happier on my current path. I continue to strive for excellence in my career and remain passionate about empowering others with financial knowledge. I'm grateful for the experiences and challenges that have shaped me, and I look forward to positively impacting the financial industry for years to come.

As I continue my journey, I'm committed to being a voice for change and an advocate for diversity and inclusion in the financial industry. My passion for financial education will continue to be the basis for conversations with any and everybody around things you don't know you don't know and generating generational wealth. Generational wealth is not just for your children, or immediate family, but for communities, extended families, friends who have become family, and those who don't have families.

To aspiring Black women who are considering a career in finance, I say: We need you! We need you in today's financial landscape, and we need your brilliance to shape tomorrow. The industry needs you, just as you are needed in so many other areas of life because we do things like only we can. Don't let the barriers discourage you. Embrace your unique perspective, harness your skills and knowledge, and strive for excellence. Seek out mentors and allies who will support and guide you along the way. And most importantly, never stop learning and growing.

My journey is far from over. I love that my story is unique and combines so many different awesome journeys that give me hope that we will continue to create a brighter and more inclusive financial future for all.

"A Journey of Resilience, Leadership, and Success"

The Jenny Flores Story

*M*Y PERSONAL AND professional journey has been one of overcoming adversity, working toward creating generational wealth, and cultivating joy throughout each step of my adventures. As an immigrant woman of color, I have definitely faced hurdles in reaching my goals. Yet, I have learned to maintain a firm hold on my vision and values, draw on my leadership abilities, and leverage my experiences to propel myself and those around me toward success. My sincere hope is that my story will serve as an example, encouraging others to surmount their personal challenges and realize their dreams.

Raised in an immigrant community in San Francisco, my formative years were about learning to survive and thrive in a completely new country and culture. The migration of my family from El Salvador to the United States when I was two and a half years old was driven by my grandfather, a successful entrepreneur who became literate as an adult and whose vision was to provide his family with a life removed from our homeland's hardships and violence. Upon settling in the vibrant city of San Francisco, I was immersed in a melting pot of immigrants who shared similar struggles and experiences. Although grappling with a language barrier myself, as a young girl, I began acting as a translator for English-challenged adults in the community. This unique role underscored the importance of effective communication and interpersonal connections, and I learned skills that I would carry forward throughout my life. My upbringing within this richly diverse community instilled in me the principle of mutual support, which allows us to transcend our disparate backgrounds. Unbeknownst to me, these early experiences laid the groundwork for my future leadership trajectory.

Years later with the support of my family, I embarked on pursuing higher education. I received a bachelor's degree in political science from the University of California, Berkeley, followed by an MBA from Babson College in Massachusetts.

As I ventured into the professional world, it was clear that the majority of individuals at the very top of the management chain did not reflect my experience at all. As a result, some of my early ideas for innovation and impact were dismissed as being too "niche" and, in their opinion, likely unprofitable. While initially discouraged by the reactions I received, I recognized these apparent setbacks as opportunities for personal growth and development. I learned that the key to success often lies in understanding the needs and motivations of others, and, by honing my empathetic communication skills, I could get much further.

Reflecting on my path to leadership, I recall how I didn't perceive myself as a leader until later in life. This realization occurred when I joined a program called Zero Divide Fellowship, where I was considered a leader among a group of seasoned professionals. It took a conversation with a colleague to understand that leadership is about having a vision, uplifting communities, uniting people, and effecting positive change. This newfound understanding of leadership was both fascinating and intimidating, as the term *leader* felt like an enormous mantle to assume.

To cultivate my leadership abilities, I turned to books on time management, strategic planning and achieving excellent execution. However, the most significant growth catalysts were the lessons learned from my numerous mentors, including lessons on the importance of authenticity, humility, staying true to your values and not being afraid to dream big and set audacious goals. One of those mentors who significantly impacted my journey was Virginia Apodaca. As a high-ranking government official, she demonstrated that women could ascend to powerful positions and succeed in them. Her assured confidence and unwavering determination were sources of inspiration, fueling my aspirations. From her, I learned the significance of self-belief, the art of understanding others' decision-making processes, and the importance of not allowing physical attributes or skin color to become barriers to success.

As I look back on my journey, three experiences profoundly influenced my path:

Embracing my leadership skills: Recognizing my potential as a leader allowed me to hone my abilities and employ them to benefit my community and effect change.

Overcoming adversity: The myriad of challenges I faced as a young immigrant in an unfamiliar land instilled resilience, determination, and the critical importance of unwavering commitment to my goals.

Learning to navigate corporate America: My journey to becoming a successful executive in banking was paved with hard work, perseverance, and a clear vision. Today, I use my experiences and insights to help others attain their dreams.

Through these experiences, I learned that failure was not a dead end but rather a detour on the road to success. As someone with a vision and goal to break the mold and chart my path, I encountered numerous rejections. But with time, I realized these perceived roadblocks were steppingstones guiding me toward refining my approach. By adopting a new perspective and seeking to understand the views of others, I turned negative encounters into lessons. I share this advice for those with grand dreams: Embrace your vision and practice stepping out of your comfort zone so fear does not immobilize you from taking the necessary steps to achieve your objectives. Also, it is important to reframe failure from a bad thing to a lesson to be learned to move forward more strategically and thoughtfully. Those insights are gold!

Throughout all these growth stages, I have been blessed to have my family by my side. The unwavering support of my mom, siblings, husband and daughter has made all the difference in my ability to achieve my goals and navigate the ups and downs of life. Aligning my core values with my work has been pivotal to my personal and professional growth along with nurturing a robust network of mentors and colleagues. I actively sought to broaden my network by attending networking events and conferences nationwide to connect with the best minds both in and outside of my field. However, the onset of the COVID-19 pandemic ushered in a new paradigm. As the world shifted to virtual platforms, I adapted my networking approach by participating in webinars, joining online communities, and attending virtual events, allowing me to connect with individuals worldwide and establish relationships that would have been otherwise impossible.

Reflecting on my journey, from an immigrant family to an executive at one of the country's largest financial institutions, I see a path marked by challenges and opportunities for growth. Amid the myriad of lessons I've gathered, one stands out: the importance of staying true to oneself. As I continue my journey, I strive to live by this principle, leading with authenticity and serving as support for others who dare to dream big.

The Unconventional CEO: Leading the Way

I Am an UnConventional CEO

*L*ET'S FACE IT, being an UnConventional CEO isn't like being a superhero. I don't get to wear a flashy cape or have a quirky sidekick, even though, at times, I wish I had both. But it does require superhuman perseverance, grit, and the ability to bounce back from failures quicker than a ping-pong ball on a hot skillet.

But here's the twist—I'm not just an UnConventional CEO. I'm a Black, disabled, lesbian UnConventional CEO, which, let's be real, is a whole different ball game. Picture it like playing a video game on the hardest level of difficulty, with all the dragons and obstacles turned up to eleven. Yet, this unique identity fuels my determination to create change and disrupt the status quo.

Starting the LEGACY! Card Game was like being thrown into the deep end without swimming lessons. I went from being a social worker—a job that, while challenging, came with its own set of guidelines and comfort zones—to navigating the choppy seas of entrepreneurship, with nothing more than an idea, a boatload of optimism, and a Kickstarter campaign.

Now, raising funds on Kickstarter is no walk in the park. It's more like climbing a mountain while blindfolded and balancing an egg on a spoon. We did it despite the odds stacked against us—given that less than half of all Kickstarter campaigns meet their funding goals. We didn't hit a million-dollar jackpot, but we raised enough to keep my dream afloat, and in the journey of entrepreneurship, every small win is a stepping stone to the next milestone. Let me take you on a behind-the-scenes tour of how we managed to pull off a successful Kickstarter campaign. I know $6,000 might not sound like a lottery win to some, but in the start-up world, every dollar counts, and for me, it was a mini jackpot. It's not just about the money but the validation and support each contribution represents.

I didn't jump into Kickstarter without doing my homework first. I dissected successful gaming campaigns like a biology student with a frog. I studied their strategies, read articles, devoured interviews, and picked the brains of successful creators. A few golden nuggets emerged from my research. I learned that a compelling video was the beating heart of a successful campaign. It was also crucial to rally the troops—friends, family, my mailman, everyone I knew—before launching the campaign. Also, it turned out that persistence in social media promotion wasn't just helpful, it was a necessity.

And here's the kicker—it's OK to start small. Our initial goal was modest, but it allowed us to test the waters. And, well, not to brag, but we sailed past it by miles, raising ten times our original goal, which helped us upgrade our product quality.

But the journey was about more than just the Kickstarter campaign. I dove into the chilly waters of cold emailing, armed with only a keyboard and my vision. I reached out to executives in the financial sector, weaving my passion into every word of the email. Amid the sea of emails, one individual emerged and chose to back our dream.

RocketReach and Apollo.io became my secret weapons, providing me with email addresses of key players in the industry. This helped me build a bridge to the people who could help propel my venture.

Building social capital was like climbing a mountain, but I learned the importance of finding your tribe. Organizations like The Nasdaq Entrepreneurial Center, Halcyon House, 2-Gether International, Goodie Nation, and the ParentPreneur Foundation became my guiding stars, offering mentorship, resources, community, and opening doors to countless opportunities. Their support, coupled with wins like the Amber Grants for Women, was a testament to the power of social capital in entrepreneurship.

Raising funds on Kickstarter was just the beginning, the first step in our journey. Our journey is about more than just a card game; it's about turning a vision into a reality. And I'm proud to say that we are well on our way with a successful Kickstarter campaign, a supportive community, and a relentless will to make a difference.

Through the ups and downs of this adventure, my mission has stayed crystal clear: to empower Black and Brown families through financial education and long-term investing. As the UnConventional CEO of Financial Joy School, I've touched the six-figure income bracket and now, I'm setting my sights on the seven-figure territory. But more than just income, my success is marked by the over twenty thousand families who have been empowered through our partnerships and are now writing their own financial success stories.

My entrepreneurial journey and the vision behind Financial Joy School have found a spot on renowned platforms like Forbes.com, Inc.com, Inc Magazine, Mashable, Roland Martin Unfiltered, Black Enterprise, Official Black Wall Street, and We Buy Black. While these features have helped amplify our mission and introduce us to a wider audience, the core goal remains to bridge the racial wealth gap and inspire Black and Brown communities to build generational wealth.

One of my most humbling achievements has been the opportunity to share my story on Wells Fargo ATM screens worldwide, a testament to the reach and impact of Financial Joy School. My journey, like any entrepreneur's, has been studded with failures. But each stumble, each rough patch, has only served to make me more tenacious and resilient.

Each milestone, each victory, amplifies my passion and reaffirms my commitment to this mission. I dream of creating a legacy of empowerment, prosperity, and financial joy for future generations. And I'm not alone in this journey. Our community's unwavering support, which believes in the transformative power of financial education, fuels our march toward our goal.

My heart swells with gratitude for every single individual who has been a part of this journey and supported Financial Joy School. Your belief in our mission is the wind beneath my wings, pushing me to scale greater heights. Together, we can shatter stereotypes and make financial empowerment a reality.

I want to express my deepest gratitude to everyone who has accompanied me on this journey. Your financial contributions, emotional support, and partnerships have significantly shaped my success and that of Financial Joy School. Every day, I'm inspired by the families we've reached, the lives we've changed, and the stories of resilience and determination that continue to pour in.

So, remember, entrepreneurship is not a cakewalk. It's a journey fraught with challenges and setbacks. But armed with unflinching faith and steadfast determination, you can overcome any hurdles that stand in your way. So never stop chasing your dreams because they can change not only your life but also the lives of those around you. Remember, the road to success is always under construction. So, keep going and never give up on your dreams.

Your Road Map to Resilience, Wealth, and Leadership: Practical Steps and Action Plans

*S*TARTING ON A path toward resilience, wealth, and leadership involves much more than a mere road map. It requires a mental shift from being a bystander in your financial life to becoming the UnConventional CEO of your destiny. This journey asks for courage, determination, and a thirst for personal growth and financial freedom. The steps below will guide you through your transformative journey, but remember, these aren't one-size-fits-all. Adapt and modify these steps as you progress on your unique path.

Embrace Your Whole Self – Warts and All:

Leadership begins with self-awareness. Engage in self-reflection to recognize your strengths, weaknesses, and passions. Acknowledge the things that bring you joy and those that challenge or frustrate you. Accepting all aspects of yourself—the good, the bad, and the "still working on it"—is the foundation of genuine leadership.

Set and Pursue Clear Goals:

The UnConventional CEO of any organization sets the vision and outlines clear goals. The same applies to you as the UnConventional CEO of your personal life. Identify your leadership, financial, and personal happiness aspirations. Create a road map with specific, achievable steps, time frames, and success measures. Bear in mind, the journey toward these goals isn't always straightforward. Goals change, timelines shift, but what counts is having the resilience and flexibility to adapt and continue moving forward.

Develop a Strategic Financial Plan:

The most effective leaders are strategic thinkers. Create a comprehensive financial plan that directs your resources toward savings, investments, and spending that align with your life goals. In developing this plan, set specific financial goals and strategize how you will achieve them.

Increase Your Financial Literacy:

A good, UnConventional CEO never stops learning. Commit to improving your financial education. Attend seminars, read finance books, follow market trends, and explore investment opportunities. Set up alerts for key phrases like "investment trends" or "financial opportunities for Black and Brown families" to stay informed. Constant learning allows you to make informed decisions, helping you maximize your financial potential.

Direct Your Money:

As we've emphasized before, you're the UnConventional CEO; you decide where your money goes. Ensure it's working toward your goals.

Build Your Board of Directors:

An UnConventional CEO surrounds themselves with a team of experts who provide advice, insights, and support. Create your personal "board of directors"—a network of like-minded individuals who share your financial aspirations and values.

This support system will provide encouragement, inspiration, and accountability as you progress toward your goals.

Hone Your Emotional Intelligence and Resilience:

Leadership is as much about emotional intelligence as it is about decision-making and strategic planning. Develop your ability to cope with setbacks, adapt to changes, and manage stress effectively. Practice self-compassion and gratitude to maintain a positive mindset and stay motivated on your journey.

Engage in Regular Financial Check-ins:

A successful UnConventional CEO regularly reviews the organization's performance. Apply this principle to your financial journey. Regularly evaluate your financial progress, assess your successes and setbacks, and adjust your plan as necessary.

Share Your Leadership Journey:

Inspire others by sharing your leadership story and financial wisdom. As you navigate your journey to close the wealth gap, you pave the way for others. Your resilience, leadership, and wealth creation story can serve as a guiding light for others striving for similar goals. Sharing your knowledge is not just a generous act; it's a contribution to the collective effort to promote financial equality and leadership growth in your community.

Live a Life of Purpose and Joy:

As you navigate your leadership journey, always align your financial plans with your values and passions. Strive to live a fulfilling, purposeful, and joy-filled life, using your financial resources to create meaningful experiences, give back to your community, and leave a legacy.

Promote Your Own Growth:

Just as an UnConventional CEO seeks out opportunities to grow the business, look for avenues to develop yourself personally and professionally. Attend seminars, enroll in leadership courses, find a mentor, or hire a coach. All these resources can equip you with the tools to hone your leadership skills and navigate your journey confidently.

Invest in Your Leadership Skills:

Spend time and resources nurturing and expanding your leadership skills. Attend leadership workshops, read books on leadership, and seek mentorship from established leaders in your field. Practice decision-making, conflict resolution, and strategic planning, and apply these skills in your daily life.

Embrace Innovation:

A forward-thinking UnConventional CEO embraces innovation. Be open to new ideas and ready to adapt to changes in your personal and financial life. Utilize technological tools and platforms that can aid in managing your finances better.

By assuming the role of UnConventional CEO in your journey toward resilience, wealth, and leadership, you are consciously steering your destiny toward financial empowerment and personal growth. Trust the process, embrace the journey, and remember that each step you take shapes a brighter future for yourself, your family, and future generations. Your journey to wealth and leadership isn't just about financial success—it's about crafting a life of purpose, joy, and enduring impact.

The Realities and Triumphs of Entrepreneurship and Leadership

MANY PEOPLE FANTASIZE about the glamorous life of being a leader, owning a business, and having control over their own destiny. However, the truth is that the journey of leadership, entrepreneurship, and building wealth can be incredibly challenging. In fact, your financial woes don't magically disappear when you step into a leadership role or start your own business. In many cases, they become amplified. Let me share a personal story from my own journey to illustrate the reality of leadership and entrepreneurship. When I first started my business, everything seemed to fall into place effortlessly. I was winning deals left and right, manufacturing my products in the USA, running a successful Kickstarter campaign, and selling my products in over forty states and five countries. I even had the privilege of being featured in reputable publications like MASHABLE and INC. Life and business were thriving, and it felt like I couldn't lose.

However, as time went on, I experienced the harsh truth of the ebb and flow of business. Deals began to dry up, opportunities that were once abundant became scarce, and my financial situation took a hit. The initial success I had enjoyed started to wane, and I found myself facing new challenges and setbacks.

In the world of leadership and entrepreneurship, you will often feel like you're never doing enough. The pressure to constantly achieve and sustain success can be overwhelming. It's important to remember that this feeling is common, and you're not alone in experiencing it. Take a moment to breathe and remind yourself that you are doing your best.

The truth is that many people fantasize about the glamorous side of leadership and entrepreneurship, the moments of triumph and abundance that are showcased on social media. We see the luxurious vacations, the new homes, the fancy cars, and all the material possessions that make it seem like success comes effortlessly. What is rarely shown, however, are the moments of decrease, the setbacks and challenges that are an integral part of the journey.

As a leader, you will face times when deals fall through, clients disappear, and the path ahead seems uncertain. The sales cycle in your industry may take months or even years to close a deal, leaving you in constant anticipation and uncertainty. The reality is that leadership and entrepreneurship can be a roller-coaster ride of feast and famine, with periods of abundance followed by periods of scarcity.

Acknowledging that not every decision you make will lead to immediate success is important. Some choices will yield incredible results, like striking oil, while others may feel like hitting dirt. The moments of hitting dirt can be disheartening and can shake your confidence, but they are an inevitable part of the process. It's during these moments that true growth and resilience are forged.

I want to share these truths with you because it's essential to approach leadership and entrepreneurship with a clear understanding of the challenges and setbacks that lie ahead. Glamorizing these roles without acknowledging the reality does a disservice to aspiring leaders and entrepreneurs. Temporary setbacks and dry seasons are a natural part of the journey, but they should not define your future or create a long-lasting impact.

Despite all these challenges, I also want to stress that leadership and entrepreneurship are still tremendously fulfilling. There are few feelings that can match the exhilaration of seeing a project you've led to fruition, or witnessing the growth of a business you started from scratch. So, if you're thinking about starting a business or already on that path, don't be deterred by the challenges. They are part of the journey, and they're what makes the successes even sweeter.

As a leader, embracing the challenges and setbacks as opportunities for growth and learning is crucial. They shape your character, build resilience, and ultimately contribute to your success. By facing the truth head-on, you can navigate the highs and lows of leadership with a grounded perspective.

So, as we embark on this journey together, let's do so with our eyes wide open, knowing that the road ahead won't always be smooth. By acknowledging the truth about being a leader, we can mentally, emotionally, and financially prepare ourselves for the inevitable ups and downs. Let's embrace reality and turn it into a source of strength and determination as we navigate the unpredictable leadership path.

Yet, the essence of entrepreneurship and leadership lies in acknowledging these realities. Remain persistent because your passion and conviction for your venture are strong enough to weather the storm. One of the greatest joys of being an entrepreneur is being able to look back at your journey, realizing how much you've grown and evolved both personally and professionally. You grow not only a business but also as a person, which is something money can't buy.

Entrepreneurship is not only about making money, gaining fame, or even realizing a dream. It's also about self-discovery, resilience, perseverance, and the ability to adapt and learn continuously. You come to understand that success isn't always measured in the currency of wealth or fame but also in lessons learned, relationships built, personal growth, and the impact you make.

Every setback, every failure is not the end but a stepping stone. Each provides a new perspective and lesson that helps you in your journey. It's OK to fail; it's OK to make mistakes. What's important is that you learn from these experiences and keep moving forward.

Facing challenges and overcoming them is part of the leadership journey. When you hit a wall, find a way around it, over it, or under it. Each challenge you overcome builds your strength and resilience. It teaches you that you are capable of much more than you thought possible. It shows you that you can withstand the pressure, the uncertainty, and the hardship and still emerge stronger.

It's also essential to remember that you are not alone as a leader. Entrepreneurship may seem like a lonely path, but it doesn't have to be. Building and nurturing relationships are crucial to this journey. Surrounding yourself with supportive people, mentors, and peers who are on a similar journey can provide the moral support you need to continue moving forward. Sharing experiences, ideas, and challenges can help you gain new insights and perspectives that can be beneficial in overcoming obstacles and challenges.

Moreover, it's important to acknowledge that you're not just building a business or leading a team. You're creating a legacy. The values you uphold, the culture you foster, and the example you set will echo in the halls of your organization and in the hearts and minds of your team members long after you've moved on.

As you continue this journey, remember to take care of your mental, emotional, spiritual, and physical health. Success in leadership or entrepreneurship includes more than financial or professional accomplishments. It also includes maintaining a balanced lifestyle. Incorporating self-care routines, finding time for leisure and relaxation, and nurturing personal relationships are just as important as business meetings and strategy sessions.

At the end of the day, the path to success is not a straight line. It's a winding road filled with bumps, curves, and dead ends. But it's also a journey filled with beautiful landscapes, unforgettable experiences, and personal growth. Embrace each part of this journey, both the challenges and the triumphs, for they are all integral parts of your story.

Remember, you don't have to have it all figured out. The journey of entrepreneurship and leadership is a continuous process of learning, adapting, and growing. You have the strength and determination to turn challenges into opportunities. Trust your journey, trust the process, and most importantly, trust yourself. Because at the end of the day, it's not just about the destination, it's about the journey.

Embracing Joy in Your Life: Understanding the Power of Your Inner Light

*L*IFE, IN ALL its complexity, has been a winding journey for me, a path speckled with obstacles and traumas that have tested my joy, resilience, and ultimately molded the woman I am today. Each hurdle, each tumultuous wave, has left a lasting imprint on my spirit, whether it was the harrowing depths of sexual abuse, the soul-shattering murder of my dear brother, or the traumatic brain injury that turned my world upside down.

Among these pivotal moments, the traumatic brain injury was a particularly stark turning point, altering my life's trajectory in profound ways. The incident was a stark reminder of my mortality and spurred a complete reevaluation of my priorities. It was amid this period of healing and self-discovery that I came to terms with a fundamental truth about myself—that I am a lesbian who deeply loves God and Yeshua. I realized that my spirituality and my sexuality could coexist in harmony, regardless of the dissonant voices from my church and family that suggested otherwise.

However, the journey didn't end there. You see, I had been a stutterer all my life, even before the traumatic brain injury. But this condition did not stop me, nor did it define me. Navigating the challenges of living with a stutter felt like carrying an additional load on an already treacherous journey. This speech impediment often made me feel voiceless, a puzzle piece that couldn't fit into the grand picture of smooth communication. But this obstacle only further steeled my resolve, demanding even more self-acceptance and steadfast dedication toward unearthing my unique voice amid the stumbling words.

From a tender age, I was thrust into a challenge that seemed insurmountable, yet through relentless perseverance and the precious support of those around me, I gradually stepped out from the penumbra of silence. I embraced my authentic self and reclaimed my power to communicate, one word, one sentence, one conversation at a time.

These experiences have shaped my perspective on life, love, joy, and acceptance. They have taught me the value of empathy, compassion, and understanding. And most importantly, they have ignited a fire within me to create a world where everyone feels joy, is seen, heard, and loved—regardless of our beliefs, identities, or circumstances.

In the depths of my personal trials, I discovered an unyielding joy that radiates from within. It is a joy that defies the darkness: it gives light to the darkness and reminds me of the resilience of the human spirit. This joy fuels my purpose-driven life and my desire to uplift and empower others, to show them that they, too can find joy and embrace their true selves despite the challenges we may face.

Today, I lie before you (because nine times out of ten, I am relaxing not standing) as a testament to the transformative power of embracing all aspects of my identities and experiences. I am a living embodiment of love, resilience, joy, and authenticity. I invite you to join me on this journey, to embrace your own unique story, and to find joy and purpose in the face of adversity. In our journey through life, we can embrace a powerful force that transcends mere emotions: JOY. Unlike happiness or sadness, joy is not an external response to circumstances but a profound state of being that we must consciously accept and nurture within ourselves. It is an intrinsic aspect of our existence, independent of external factors. Today, we embark on a quest to explore the true nature of joy and its significance in our lives while also delving into the vital role resilience plays in our ability to embrace and sustain joy.

Defining Joy (Ruby's Dictionary)

To fully grasp the essence of joy, we must differentiate it from happiness. While happiness is often fleeting and dependent on external stimuli, joy remains unwavering and resides within us. It is not subject to the ups and downs of life, nor is it tied to temporary moments of gratification. Joy is a deep-rooted state of being that endures even in the face of adversity. By understanding this distinction, we liberate ourselves from pursuing external happiness and tap into the wellspring of everlasting fulfillment that joy offers.

The Foundation of Joy and Resilience

At the core of joy lies a fundamental belief in our purpose and the greater good we contribute to this world. It is the unwavering conviction that our lives hold significance and that our actions and choices are inextricably connected to our purpose and the betterment of society. Understanding this truth lays a solid foundation for joy to flourish within us.

Moreover, it is through resilience that we can navigate the challenges and setbacks that life presents. Resilience is the inner strength that enables us to bounce back, adapt, and find joy even in the face of adversity. By cultivating resilience, we become better equipped to embrace and sustain joy throughout life's ups and downs.

Crafting Your Personal Joy Statement

To further solidify our connection to joy and resilience, YOU can create a personal joy statement that embodies our individual beliefs and values. Drawing on our spirituality (or not), personal experiences, and our faith in a higher power or in ourselves, we can craft a statement that serves as a constant reminder of our resilience and commitment to joy. This statement acts as a guiding light during challenging times, reminding us of our inner strength and the unwavering presence of joy within us.

Here is my JOY STATEMENT: *"Everything that has happened to me has been for my greater good. The more intense the trauma, the greater the disappointment and the deeper the pain, the more profound my sense of purpose becomes, and the greater my JOY.*

It is not because I had to suffer; it is because we had to heal. Joy is not merely an emotion; it is a state of being. This joy that I possess is not something bestowed on me by the world, and it cannot be taken away by the world.

Joy is the embracing of my truth, the truth that God, the higher power, created me with intention, desiring me to be a part of this vast world. Because of this truth, I am validated, as God himself has validated me.

God has validated me because he loves me, and his love has no beginning or end. His love is infinite and boundless. Such is his love for me that he has bestowed on me an unlimited amount of grace and favor through my Savior. Even in my missteps and failures, I will continue to grow.

When I continuously embrace these truths, I am not only embracing and accepting the presence of joy in my life but also acknowledging its unwavering presence no matter what challenges I may face.

Whether my business deals fail or succeed, whether cash is flowing abundantly or drying up like a desert, whether my body is strong and capable or weak and frail, whether I receive yeses or noes in life, I still possess joy because I choose to embrace it. Joy becomes my constant companion, guiding me through the ebbs and flows of life, reminding me of the resilience and strength that lie within."

3 KEYS TO EMBRACING JOY

#1 – Create your own JOY STATEMENT

#2 – Embracing Joy in Life's Journey:

Life is an ever-changing journey, filled with highs and lows, triumphs and tribulations. Embracing joy during life's uncertainties is a testament to our resilience and unwavering spirit. We explore practical strategies for cultivating joy, such as practicing gratitude, embracing self-care, nurturing meaningful connections, and finding purpose in our daily pursuits. By integrating these practices into our lives, we create a resilient foundation that allows joy to flourish and sustain us through life's inevitable challenges.

#3 – The Power of Resilience in Embracing Joy: Resilience acts as the bridge that connects us to joy. We delve deeper into the characteristics and mindset of resilient individuals, understanding how they overcome obstacles, adapt to change, and find joy even in the face of adversity. We uncover the power of resilience in transforming setbacks into opportunities for growth and discover the profound joy that comes from navigating life's challenges with grace and perseverance.

By embracing the essence of joy in life and cultivating resilience, we unlock the potential to lead fulfilling and resilient lives. Joy becomes a steadfast companion that uplifts us even in the darkest moments, while resilience empowers us to navigate life's uncertainties with grace, determination, and action. Joy and resilience form a powerful synergy, enabling us to continuously embrace life's journey and live authentically, purposefully, and with joy. Got joy? I hope so!

Resources for Financial Education, Mentorship, and Entrepreneurial Support

*E*MBARKING ON A journey toward financial empowerment requires access to reliable resources, guidance from experienced mentors, and a supportive community to help you stay accountable and motivated. In this chapter, we will introduce you to various resources for financial education, mentorship, and support that can assist you in building wealth and achieving your financial goals.

As we near the end of this book, I want to leave you with some valuable resources for your financial education, mentorship, and entrepreneurial support. Embarking on a journey toward financial empowerment requires access to reliable resources, guidance from experienced mentors, and a supportive community to help you stay accountable and motivated.

In this chapter, I have listed some books, podcasts, websites, and platforms that can assist you in building wealth and achieving your financial goals. These resources provide insights into the history of Black wealth, success stories of Black millionaires, and practical advice on building wealth tailored to the Black community's unique experiences and challenges. They also cover various financial topics, from investing and personal finance to entrepreneurship and wealth-building strategies, offering valuable insights and advice from experts and successful individuals in the field.

Furthermore, I have shared some platforms that allow you to open a brokerage account, buy stocks and mutual funds, and manage your investment portfolio. Each platform has its unique features and fees, so research and choose the one that best suits your needs and preferences.

Lastly, I have provided web addresses for several entrepreneurial support organizations that can help you succeed in your endeavors and create a lasting impact in your communities. These organizations provide resources, mentorship, and support for entrepreneurs, helping them gain the knowledge, skills, and support necessary to navigate the world of personal finance and wealth building effectively.

By leveraging these resources, you can empower yourself to make informed decisions, set achievable financial goals, and work toward a brighter financial future for yourself and your family. Remember, building wealth is a journey, not a destination.

Embarking on a journey toward financial empowerment requires access to reliable resources, guidance from experienced mentors, and a supportive community to help you stay accountable and motivated. In this chapter, we will introduce you to various resources for financial education, mentorship, and support that can assist you in building wealth and achieving your financial goals.

Books to Read

History of the Black Dollar by Angel Rich
Think and Grow Rich: A Black Choice by Dennis Kimbro and
    Napoleon Hill
Why Should White Guys Have All the Fun? by Reginald Lewis
The Wealth Choice: Success Secrets of Black Millionaires by
    Dennis Kimbro

These books provide insights into the history of Black wealth, success stories of Black millionaires, and practical advice on building wealth tailored to the Black community's unique experiences and challenges.

Podcasts to Listen to:

Financial Joy School Podcast
Market Mondays
Rule Breaker Investing – A Motley Fool Podcast
Brown Ambition with Mandi and Tiffany
While Black
Your First Million by Arlan Hamilton
Better with Paul
Tropical
SPORTS CARD INVESTORS

These podcasts cover a range of financial topics, from investing and personal finance to entrepreneurship and wealth-building strategies. They offer valuable insights and advice from experts and successful individuals in the field.

Websites to Visit

Financial Joy School: https://FinancialJoySchool.com
The Black Wall Streeter: https://www.theblackwallstreet-er. com/welcome

Investopedia: A comprehensive resource for financial information, Investopedia offers articles, tutorials, and tools on a wide range of financial topics. https://www. investopedia.com

Freeman Capital: https://freemancapital.co
The Penny Hoarder: https://www.thepennyhoarder.com
Get Wealthy Life: https://www.getwealthylife.com
Magnify Money: http://MagnifyMoney.com
Legacy Card Game: https://LegacyCardGame.com

These websites offer a wealth of information on personal finance, investing, wealth-building strategies, and tools and resources to help you make informed financial decisions.

How to buy mutual funds and stocks, and where to open a brokerage account:

Fidelity: https://Fidelity.com
Vanguard: https://investor.vanguard.com/my-account/ log-on
Robinhood: https://Robinhood.com
Acorns: https://www.acorns.com/

These platforms allow you to open a brokerage account, buy stocks and mutual funds, and manage your investment portfolio. Each platform has its unique features and fees, so research and choose the one that best suits your needs and preferences.

Here are the web addresses for the entrepreneurial support organizations mentioned in the previous response:

1. Nasdaq Entrepreneurial Center:
    https://thecenter.nasdaq.org/
2. Halcyon House: https://halcyonhouse.org/
3. Goodie Nation: https://goodienation.org/
4. 2Gether International:
    https://2gether-international.org/
5. ParentsPreneur Foundation:
    https:// www.parentpreneurfoundation.org/

These organizations provide resources, mentorship, and support for entrepreneurs, helping them succeed in their endeavors and create lasting impact in their communities.

By leveraging these resources, you can gain the knowledge, skills, and support necessary to navigate the world of personal finance and wealth building effectively. These tools can empower you to make informed decisions, set achievable financial goals, and work toward a brighter financial future for yourself and your family.

My Resilience, Sunshine, and a Personal Mission for Change

AS WE TAKE the last steps of our shared journey through this book, I encourage you to reflect. Reflect on resilience, the core of our power that keeps us striving despite the blows of life. Reflect on the warmth and light of joy, the sunshine we've found even in the darkest days. Reflect on the mission we've discussed—the pursuit of not just personal wealth but a larger vision of societal equity and generational prosperity. It's our shared journey of hope, learning, and transformation that binds us all.

Remember that financial resilience, wealth building, and joy do not exist in silos. They intertwine, and the power of community can amplify their essence. Often, we choose to navigate our financial paths alone, but the shared wisdom and resources of a community can make the journey less daunting and more enriching. Success is sweeter when it's shared, and the fruits of financial freedom taste best when enjoyed in a community.

You're not alone on this journey. Remember that. We share a collective pursuit of financial freedom and well-being. We all face trials, overcome hurdles, and celebrate victories. By promoting open discussions about money and sharing our experiences and lessons, we can uplift each other and nurture a community where financial well-being is accessible to all.

Adversity isn't always a pitfall. It can be a stepping stone, a push toward growth. Tap into your inner resilience when faced with financial setbacks. Every challenge is a lesson, and every lesson takes you one step closer to your financial goals. And through this journey, never lose sight of joy. It's the sunshine that brightens the gloomiest of days, the force that keeps us motivated and optimistic.

As you pave the path for generational wealth, creating a legacy for your family, remember to celebrate every milestone, no matter how small. The journey toward financial freedom isn't a straight one; it's a road marked by twists and turns, ups and downs. Your achievements are markers of your resilience, reminders of how far you've come.

Finally, pay it forward. Knowledge is most beneficial when it's shared. Empower those around you with your wisdom your experiences. Your contribution can help shape a world where financial equity is a reality, not a distant dream.

As I reach the closing lines of this book, akin to a Baptist pastor bidding farewell to his congregation, I reflect on my journey. I have been molded by resilience, inspired by sunshine, and motivated by a mission. This mission isn't just about personal success; it's about creating a world of financial equality. It's about making financial literacy a right, not a privilege. It's about dismantling generational poverty and building bridges to financial empowerment.

My path hasn't been easy, and I know the road ahead will test my resolve. But with every challenge I overcome and every person I empower, I move closer to my vision: a world where the racial wealth gap is history, where financial freedom is a universal reality.

This book is a testament to the resilience that helped me conquer my darkest days, the sunshine that fueled my optimism, and my unwavering pursuit of a future marked by equity and prosperity. As I embark on the mission of narrowing the racial wealth gap, these lessons will serve as my beacon, guiding , inspiring , and reminding me of my power to effect change.

Let's join hands in this mission, igniting a wave of transformation that transcends our personal goals. Together, we can create an equitable world where wealth isn't just about material abundance, but a legacy of fairness and opportunities passed down through generations. Let's strive for a world radiant with opportunities, where the brightness touches every corner and reaches every individual, no matter their origin. This is our collective mission and our shared journey. We have the power to effect change, to write our own narratives, and to shape the world we leave behind for the next generation.

We stand on the precipice of a new era—one marked by financial equality, prosperity, and hope. As we step into this new chapter, let's carry with us the lessons we've learned, the resilience we've cultivated, and the joy we've discovered along the way.

As you close this book and move forward on your financial journey, remember that this is not an end, but a beginning. Embrace the challenge ahead with courage, fueled by the knowledge that you can overcome adversity and create lasting change.

Keep the light of resilience and joy in your heart. Let it guide you through the stormy seas, light your path in the darkest nights, and remind you of the sunny days that lie ahead. As you navigate your path to financial freedom, keep learning, growing, and sharing. Your journey can inspire others and be the beacon they need to find their own path.

Your story of resilience and financial empowerment can ignite a spark in others. By sharing your journey, you're not only creating a legacy for yourself, but you're also empowering others to start their own journey toward financial freedom. This is the ripple effect of your actions, and it can lead to a wave of change that transforms communities and societies for the better.

As we march forward, let the sunshine of hope and resilience light our way, illuminating the path toward a more just and prosperous future for all. With resilience, determination, and a community united in its mission, we can overcome any obstacle, break any barrier, and achieve our dreams.

May this book be the spark that ignites your journey toward financial resilience, wealth, and joy. May the legacy you leave be one of hope, opportunity, and prosperity for generations to come. Keep shining, keep thriving, and most importantly, keep believing in the power of resilience and the promise of a brighter tomorrow.

In the end, remember that our combined efforts can transform the world. Our collective resilience is more potent than any adversity. Together, we can turn the tide and create a world where financial success is within reach for all. A world where the wealth gap is a thing of the past, where each person has the chance to create their own sunshine.

Let this be your call to action. Embrace resilience, pursue wealth, and always find your sunshine. You hold the power to change your life and the lives of those around you. Stand tall, walk purposefully, and let your journey be a beacon of hope for others. Be the change you wish to see in the world, and may your resilience, sunshine, and wealth inspire a brighter, more prosperous world for all.

Together, we can move mountains, bridge gaps, and create a world that is rich not only in material wealth but also in resilience, joy, and equity. A world where the sunshine touches everyone, where the wealth is shared, and where every individual, irrespective of their race or background, can thrive. This is my mission. This is our mission.

Let's take that first step together. Here's to resilience, sunshine, and a brighter future for all. Here's to closing the racial wealth gap. Here's to us. Here's to becoming an UnConventional CEO.

About the Author

RUBY "SUNSHINE" TAYLOR, MSW, is the CEO and founder of Financial Joy School, a virtual educational platform and gaming company. It provides financial education and investment tools to Black and Brown youth and their families. Ruby is a double HBCU alumna (Howard University and Virginia Union University) and advocates for closing the racial wealth gap to make our world more financially equitable. She harnesses the power of financial knowledge to bring connections, application, and education to establish generational wealth for Black families. A traumatic brain injury survivor, Ruby is a disabled Black, queer woman, wife, mother, daughter, aunt, sister, and friend who is driven to make our world more equal, joyful, and just. She is a motivational speaker and has partnered with financial brands, including Wells Fargo, and has been featured in several leading publications, including The Motley Fool, Inc. com, *Fast Company*, Mashable.com and more.

Originally from the Bronx, New York, Ruby resides in Baltimore, Maryland, with her wife, Dr. Sheila Graham, and two children.

Websites

Https://FinancialJoySchool.com
Https://LegacyCardGame.com

Social Links

TikTok @FinancialJoySchool
Instagram @FinancialJoySchool
LinkedInhttps://www.linkedin.com/in/rubytaylor
Twitter @FinancialJoy21

Venture & Impact

Financial Joy School is a financial education platform and gaming company that aims to close the racial wealth gap by providing diverse financial education, games, and investment tools to Black and Brown youth and our families.

Financial Joy School is a community of almost two thousand Black and Brown families. We have partnered with Wells Fargo and the Nasdaq Entrepreneurial Center to donate ten thousand LEGACY! Card Decks to LMI Income youth and families. We partnered with twelve non-profit organizations and public schools, such as Black Girls Smile, The Mount Washington School, Dent Education, Black Fathers Foundation, Lancaster Teenage Girl Summit, The Artest Foundation, Harlem Academy, Portfolios with Purpose, African Diaspora Alliance, and Detroit Public Schools to distribute the card games and offer financial workshops and tournaments.

We use their card game LEGACY to bring families together and teach them about investing and wealth building.

To date, the school has helped over twenty thousand families, with the goal of helping millions more.

Acknowledgments

MY PROFOUND GRATITUDE goes to my ancestors, family, friends, and mentors who have steadfastly stood by me throughout this journey. I am equally grateful to God, whose endless love and guidance have been my anchor every step of the way.

I extend my special thanks to my parents, Martin and Arline Taylor. They have been instrumental in shaping my character by instilling in me the values of faith, family, and love. Their unwavering support and encouragement have defined who I am today.

Thank you to the amazing contributors who shared their stories and light: Tomeka Brown, Arline Taylor, and Chantel Roche.

Finally, to all the readers of this book, it is my fervent hope that it arms you with the knowledge, inspiration, and tools needed to attain financial empowerment, thereby paving the way for a brighter future for you and your community. Blessings on your journey.

DISCLAIMER

Any opinions expressed in this book are those of the respective authors and not of Financial Joy School or any of its partners and/or affiliates and may differ or be contrary to opinions expressed by other business areas or groups of Financial Joy School as a result of using different assumptions and criteria. The reader should not construe the contents of this book as any legal, tax, accounting, regulatory or other specialist or technical advice, or services or investment advice, or a personal recommendation from Financial Joy School. Financial Joy School makes no representation or warranty, either express or implied, in relation to the accuracy, completeness, or reliability of the information contained herein.

Neither Financial Joy School nor any of its partners, or their respective directors, officers, employees or agents accept any liability for any loss or damage arising out of the use of all or any part of this book or reliance on the information contained herein.

Financial Joy School LLC, its affiliates and its employees do not provide tax or legal advice. You should consult with your personal financial, tax and/or legal advisor regarding your personal situation.

Printed in the USA
CPSIA information can be obtained
at www.ICGtesting.com
CBHW060711121223
2581CB00006B/29